CW01456117

Blackburn - In Their Own Words
Volume 1

Heritage Publications

First Edition 2012
Copyright Heritage Publications, 2012
ISBN 978-0-9572604-6-7

www.HeritagePublications.co.uk

Blackburn - In Their Own Words

Foreword

In 2008 and 2009 we conducted a number of interviews with people living in and around Blackburn.

In this era of digital communications, many of our own stories are being preserved every time we use devices such as computers. The children of the 1910s, 1920s, 1930s and 1940s had no such way of telling their stories, which during times of war and poverty, hold important lessons for us all. In this book, we record some fascinating stories about Blackburn and the people that have made it.

Tom Kennedy, Ada Thomas, Vincent Gibson, Bill Entwistle, Howard Talbot, Joan Bell, John Murphy, Elizabeth Stancliffe and Jim Whittle told us their memories of the town as it used to be. These stories provide us with a fascinating personal insight into Blackburn's past. This book chronicles the town that these locals lived in as they grew up, of the people they knew and the places that they visited. Some people tell of their struggles in times of war and decline, whilst others tell of happier times and prosperity. Most importantly, however, they all record their stories, not through a historian, but *In Their Own Words*.

We would like to thank all of the people that we interviewed and the relatives and loved ones of the late Tom Kennedy, Ada Thomas and Bill Entwistle. We thoroughly enjoyed meeting and talking with each of you.

We could not fit all of the interviews that we conducted into one book so we will release a second volume in the imminent future. The interviews that we have lined up for volume two are equally as memorable and remarkable as those in this volume – so please do look out for this volume. Further information on this second volume can be found at www.HeritagePublications.co.uk.

Heritage Publications

Table of Contents

Blackburn - In Their Own Words

Tom Kennedy

Born 1928

What part of the town were you born in Tom?

In the Bastwell area, 4 Palm Street. It's all completely built over now. I lived there until I got married. We overlooked the convent wall. The perimeter wall was at the back of our house.

What was the name of the convent?

The Convent of Notre Dame. My sister went there. You had to pass your scholarship to go there, like St Mary's College. It would have been about 1936.

One of the things I remember most was at the bottom of the street there was a pickle factory. It was nowhere near a factory!

The end terraced house had a slate built garage attached to it. The owner would recruit little lads in the area to work, peeling the onions, cutting up the cauliflower and gherkins for the piccalilli. My mother could always tell what we'd been doing on that day. If my hands were red it was beetroot. If they were yellow it was piccalilli. That included

round my mouth too! Peeling the onions was the worst job. Our eyes would be streaming.
How old were you at this time?
About eleven.

What was the name of the pickle firm?
No name! I can't remember the name of the man who ran the business but it was probably the most unhygienic operation you could imagine. There were no washing facilities and no toilet. You came straight from the street with dirty hands and started work. The pay was coppers plus a bonus and as many onions that you could eat. You could also take a jar home for free.
Being mindful that young boys are notorious nose pickers, what brand name or details did they put on their labels?
None. He used to have a two wheel cart with sections for the jars and he'd hawk them round the streets, cobbled streets, on a handcart he'd made himself. It was a two shafted wooden float with two old motorcycle wheels. He even had the local Coop on his rounds - for cash in hand of course! There were no such things as receipts and that's how he bought his supplies too.
Another little job we used to do for money and in kind was on Percival Street just off Whalley Range. There was a Tizer factory. I think it was the first factory that Tizer opened

with proper machinery and so on. I went
there screwing the tops on the bottles. We
used a small ratchet like device that fitted in
the palm of the hand. We would get coppers
for this but the bonus was you would get as
much Tizer as you could drink. That used to
leave a nice orange mark around your mouth
too. Your mum could always tell that you
hadn't been in trouble that day, you had been
at Tizer.

*Tizer and raw onions seems a deadly
combination!*

Yes if a competition ever came up for making
the most wind I'd have won with honours.

Laughs.

Happy days!

How many worked at the Tizer plant?

It had a small work force. I think the company
might have had their origins in Liverpool? It
was a very well organised company though as
far as the processing was concerned. The stuff
used to come in big carboys. It was a syrupy
consistency and water was added. They must
have made a fortune. I was about twelve
when I worked at the Tizer factory.

You took the Eleven Plus examination at
eleven. A few of my mates, we still meet and
talk together, and I was saying that we failed
St Mary's College on purpose. Nobody in
their right mind would want to go to school

till they are sixteen. We were all looking forward to leaving at fourteen and getting a job. It never occurred to us that we weren't clever enough to go to St Mary's.
Laughs.
When I went to school it was run by Catholic priests. They ran it with an iron hand. That was another reason I didn't want to go! Some of the priests were well known for being strict disciplinarians. Spud Murphy was the prime mover of that organisation. Out of a class of about forty kids, six would pass their Eleven Plus. The rest would go to what they called a higher grade. That was a secondary school and lot easier. That was still there for many years.
What school is this Tom?
St Alban's juniors. Then I went up to St Alban's senior boys.

Can you remember any of your teachers' names?

In the infants there were two sisters who taught. They were the Gregson sisters. Mrs Cottom was the headmistress. Then when I moved up to St Alban's junior boys I remember Mr Atkinson and Mr Stanway. The most memorable one was Mr Atkinson. He was in the Home Guard and he was an Old Contemptible, but he was rather different from most of the Old Contemptibles as he was an officer, with the wings. He was a flying officer with the Royal Flying Corps. I remember him on parade. He used to look immaculate and he had a revolver and a Sam Brown. None of the others had anything like that.

You were in the Army Cadets weren't you Tom?

You had to be fourteen to join. I kept asking my dad could I join. He gave me one of his sayings.

"I wouldn't join a bloody football club after what I've been in!" he'd say, or, "I wouldn't join the Coop!"

My dad served in the Great War. I was only thirteen then. I kept asking my dad if I could join. So I imitated dad's signature on the forms. He was a shocking writer like me and had the same initials, T Kennedy. I managed to scratch this on the form and the first day I got the uniform I thought *now then how the hell am I going to get this back home?* Anyhow I got back home and thought I'd try shock tactics and I put the uniform on.

"Oh you do look bonny in that," my mum said.

Well I thought *that's the first obstacle over with!*

"Why you barmy bugger," my dad said. "You've gone and done it!"

Anyway he got used to it eventually. These were the happiest days of my life. I was in the cadets for four years. At eighteen I joined the East Lancs Regiment. Then I was later transferred to the Royal Artillery. The war ended whilst I was in the army.

Our first headquarters were in Water Street which isn't there anymore. It ran along side the Blakewater. The building was an old billiard hall. That's where they had their headquarters for drilling and lessons. Then we went to Cardwell Place which also isn't there now. Then we went to Canterbury Street barracks. That was a great place.

When I went into the army I went up to Carlisle, which was full of Lancashire Regiments. There I did six weeks basic training. Then I went to Northern Ireland. This was in 1945/46. The troubles in Ireland hadn't resurfaced at this time, but it was just about on the boil.

We got issued with rifles. One or two days after the fitters came in to put racks all the way down the middle of the barrack room to put each rifle in. They then attached a chain through each one as the IRA were known to want these guns. That was the first indication that we were in a different country.

After Northern Ireland I was transferred to Gibraltar. Now that was heaven - sunshine and free fags.

How did you manage to get free fags?
Well when you were on active service, even though we weren't very active, they would come round every Saturday morning and throw a tin of fifty cigarettes onto your bed. I was on Gib for two years.
And you've had a bad chest ever since.
Laughs.
Did you stay on Gibraltar or venture over the border to La Linea?
Some did but it was full of knocking shops.
Laughs.
We'll say no more about that!

Tell me about your dad Tom.
Dad was unique really. He was in the oyster trade. He sold oysters nothing else. I often look back and think how could he have possibly made a living? But they were popular then. Nowadays nobody can afford them, only wealthy people. My dad used to sell them at three for half a crown.

What sort of people would buy oysters off your father?
Purely working class people. The betting fraternity were very keen on them. My dad had a lot of them in the shop together with the boozing fraternity. Beer and oysters really went together. They used to come in the shop to see how many they could eat.

Where was the shop situated Tom?

Do you remember the Grosvenor pub? The old market square? It was on the perimeter of that. I can't remember the first time I ever had an oyster. I was brought up on them.

As someone who has never fancied eating oysters, do they literally slide down your throat or do you need to chew them?

There's more fallacies talked about oysters than anything else! The biggest one is that you just swallow them. They couldn't be more wrong! The oyster is a sack, a little package, a parcel. When you penetrate that sack the liquid inside flows out into your mouth. If it's bad you spit it out because if it's bad you will know it! No matter how many you eat or have eaten, as soon as you have had a bad one, by gum you'll spit it out! So if you swallow them and they burst in your stomach through natural digestion, then the damage is done. It's too late. So I was always brought up to chew them.

Where did your dad obtain his oysters?

The common one was from Brightlingsea in Essex but the ones that the toffs would eat were a Colchester Native. The best quality Natives were a shilling each which was a lot of money and much smaller so they were considered to be less value because of this, but by gum they were different and they were good!

It's difficult to imagine now that working class people all sat around the dinner table chewing oysters.

In my dad's shop he had one small table which could accommodate two people, one at either side then it were full. My dad used to do dances at King George's Hall. There used to be a lot of functions then: The Automobile Association; the R.O.F; and Newman's Slipper Factory. He would have a little pitch in a convenient point of the hall or on top of the stairs near the entrance to the hall. A caretaker would put a couple of tables out for him for plates etcetera and off we'd go. He'd make enough in one night for as much as he'd make in the shop in four weeks. People would pop out of the ballroom for the oysters and he'd be serving all night.

A big money spinner was the Masonic Association as they had the money. My dad wasn't a mason but he was the only oyster man in town. We used to go to Samlesbury Hall and places like that and he would put his prices up. His attitude was they've got it this lot and they'll have to pay!

I remember one night in particular at Samlesbury Hall. It was a Masonic function, organised by the top of the toffs, the big wheels. We took a lot of oysters and hired a taxi to bring them and us in as we had no car in them days. We used Silverline Taxis. When we were going it was foggy. It took us a long time to get there. Eventually we arrived and we set the tables up and everything was ready for the event but nobody turned up! One or two men were seen to saunter in eventually but by 10:30pm we hadn't moved a mussel. *Laughs.*

So we opened all the oysters up and put them on six to a plate with a little piece of lemon in the middle. The whole lot were set out on this table but only about six people showed up. About two or three bought oysters, which would barely cover the taxi fare. The chap who was in charge of the event came over to my dad.

"Well Tommy it's a terrible neet ta neet and it looks like you've come unstuck with this lot," he said.

"No I haven't come unstuck!" my dad said.

"Well who's going to pay for this lot?"

"You are. Just get your cheque book out and do me a cheque!"

"Well what are you going to do with all these oysters?"

"Oh that's no problem," said my dad. "I'll eat them. I'll tell you what give us a lift!"

So we started to eat them and as I ate them I put the shells to one side and when I counted up I'd got through seventy six! That was £4 odd!

Laughs.

So a good night's trading and eating with a tasty cheque to finish off!

Yes. Apparently most of the guests were from the Chatburn and Ribble Valley area. There was no way they could have made it in that fog.

What year was this Tom?

About 1951 or 1952 when I had just got married!

Laughs.

How long was your dad in the oyster business?

All his life. Then the shop was bought over his head. He had paid rent all his life to a big London company. Then he got word that the shop had been sold to Littlewoods. My dad canvassed all the shop owners in the area and they were about a dozen. The idea was to present a plan but it was hopeless. They hadn't a chance where big money was concerned. They got their notice to quit. Fortunately dad was coming up to retirement and so it worked out ok.

Tell me about the old fish market.

There were about a dozen stalls. Six down one side and six down the other. My dad's predecessors had been fishmongers and they had a stall on the fish market.

In 1914 my dad went into the army and the stall remained vacant until the Second World War. Dad paid the rent because these stalls were like gold. The rents in those days were practically nothing, but you could put your name down for a stall and wait ages for one to come vacant. Not just on the fish market anywhere on Blackburn market. Anyway he kept it vacant all that time.

Before I went in the army I had a job in the fish market at Tomlinson's, which was a well known and respected firm. I got a job there and did about four years from being fourteen to eighteen, learning the game. So by the time the stall was ready for me I was proficient but then I had to go in the army. My dad thought that bad luck had struck again and he'd been paying for the stall for nowt - but he didn't. A chap had just been discharged out of the army. Being a fishmonger my dad contacted him to take the stall over on the understanding that when Tommy comes back it's his again. He wouldn't be fired, nothing like that, but he'd have to look around for something else. My dad would never fire an old soldier.

Thankfully by the time I was demobilised Frank had looked around and set his stall out. He'd got a business out of town. I can't remember where but it was a fish and fruit business. He did very well. I took over then.

Can you remember some of the other fish merchants on the market then Tom?
Yes, I can.

Tomlinson's of course were the main ones. They had about six stalls and about twelve staff. I don't like to harp on this too much but they had the Catholic trade as Friday's were always fish days then.

Mayer's. They had two fish stalls and they had a lot of the Freemasonry trade. You would get a lot of Freemasons going there in those days.

The others picked up the bits and pieces of trade that were left over.

Laughs.

Oh Newham's was another one.

Mac Fisheries who were nationwide. They were never a threat to the local retailer though with being such a big firm. The staff couldn't care less whether they made money or not. They had to make money of course or they'd be fired. But as far as bending over to serve a customer, being polite and so on, they got a wage anyway!

This is always the view of a smaller trader when forced to compete with a much larger organisation isn't it? The small operator has to provide that much extra customer care. It's sad don't you think that there is only one fish stall on Blackburn Market now[1]?

Yes it is. There's some characters among the old fishmongers. They were real characters and hard men. Whilst they were polite they could only take so much! They would give backchat to difficult customers without seeming offensive. I remember one old guy in particular who smoked a pipe. They didn't bother too much about health and safety. I remember this woman coming back obviously irate.

"You remember that fish you sold mi on Wednesday?"

"Aye."

"Well it were rotten!"

"Give o'er."

"I'm bloody telling yer it were rotten!"

So he thought about it for a bit then said:

"When did thee buy it?"

"WEDNESDAY!"

"Ooh I know now," he said.

"What do yer mean yer know now?"

"Tha should have bowt it Tuesday. It were alreet then!"

Laughs.

---

[1] *At the time of this interview the new market had not yet opened.*

20

Where would you buy your fish from?
I used to go for my fish to the fish hill. It's gone now but it was at the back of Morrison's supermarket on the railway sidings. I think the sidings could still be there. You would walk up by the side of what became the Boulevard pub. There was an entrance to the railway.

The wholesale fish market was a collection of shacks. A real tumbledown place. The engine would come from Fleetwood or Hull direct to the market and five stone boxes of fish would be unloaded and laid out for sale for the retailers to come and look at. They were right old timers in there. There were a lot of chip shops then. Proper fish and chip shops.

One old timer boasted: "You'll geet no bones in the fish I've filletec!"

So you'd take him on and say: "How do you make that out?"

"Well thee geet a fillet off me and see."

"But how can you guarantee that?"

"I'll show thee!"

So he'd pick a fillet up and put it to his mouth sliding it along his teeth picking out the bones.

"That why," he'd say.

Laughs.

So the chip shop proprietors and fish stall owners would come here every day?

Yes, but you couldn't buy any less than a stone in weight. For instance, a stone of cod or haddock. For the stall I'd get a more varied selection - five stone in each box. Then after they had been filleted you would take them back - usually in a bucket. The pieces would then be cut up into four portions for sale on the stall.

What do you think about the way the fish is presented in supermarkets locally?

A look of distain filled Tom's face especially when one particular outlet was mentioned!

I can really recommend the stall on the market. It is first class!

Do you still eat oysters Tom? If so how do you eat them?

I like them with vinegar and pepper, but they're very hard to open. Not everybody can open them. When I think about my dad who was in the business all his life, he would open two hundred while someone had opened three! You need a short knife that wouldn't bend with a stubby little handle on. The handle on one side should be planed off so that it fits into your hand.

Tell me about the market when you were there.

I could handle it alright as I had good training. The market superintendent, when I first started, was Mr Peel. He was an autocratic sort of bloke. In those days this sort of job was a job for life. He treated his staff firmly as he did with his tenants.

After Mr Peel we got Mr Morris. He was more of a man's man who had served in the RAF. I think that he remained there until his death.

You told me a story about a fishmonger on the outside market and the problems of leaving a busy stall even when nature called!
Laughs.

Tommy Skyles. He didn't like to leave his stall in case he lost a customer. He was a fishmonger who didn't want to be away from his stall for a minute. I shouldn't have mentioned his name. He'd be bursting but he wouldn't leave to go to the toilet so what he used to do was, he'd be standing behind the stall which came up to his chest, and he'd open his flies and start the motion.

At the same time shouting: "Nice hake or plaice. Have a look at this fish. Nice hake or plaice!"

At the same time his hands would be beckoning customers over to his stall.
Laughs.

It wouldn't be noticeable as the traders were hosing down all the time so the floor was also wet.
Laughs.

*Unless of course someone shouted there's a
fire behind your stall Tommy!*
Laughs.
Tommy was only small and like many small
people he was a belligerent little bugger. He
was one of the few to have a car. This was
parked up behind the Borough Hotel which is
now a Chinese restaurant. About this time
parking in town was getting worse. Anyway
he had this car, a little Morris Minor Traveller.
On finishing work one day he went over to
the car park, got in his car and started the
engine, but he had a wagon in front and one
behind him.
"Get the f*** out of the way!" he shouted at
one of the wagon drivers.
This is how Tommy told it: "This bloke
uncoiled himself from his wagon and he came
over slowly to me and said: 'wind your
window down' which I did and then he said:
'What did you say?'"
Tommy said: "Oh I was just thinking if you'd
like to let me out?"
Laughs.
A change of tune when this bloody mountain
came walking over to him.
Laughs.

What pubs did you go in Tom?
I went in the Borough when I was younger
and the Golden Lion. The landlady in the

Blackburn - In Their Own Words

Borough was Mrs Kitson. In the Crown Hotel it was Mrs Earnshaw. This was in the early 1950s.

The Golden Lion was a very popular pub and I'll tell you a story about this pub. My uncle was a bouncer or doorman at the pub, a real handy lad with lots of medals for swimming and weightlifting. But he also had the attitude for handling drunks and trouble makers. The Golden Lion was on the front of Church Street and there was a passage connecting the Golden Lion right through the buildings coming out on King William Street. King William Street had the longest frontage with three doors. They were the vaults, a better class vault, a middle class vault and a rough vault all connected by this passage on the main Golden Lion pub.

The landlord came through the passage to where my Uncle Steve was working on the front.

"There's trouble," the landlord said. "Come through and sort this bloke out."

So Steve grabbed him opened the door and bunged him out onto the pavement. A little later Uncle Steve was called to one of the other doors and it was the same bloke causing trouble again. He was grabbed and thrown out onto the pavement again.

A little later there was more commotion and it was this bloke yet again so Steve grabbed him

25

and threw him out of another bar onto the pavement before clocking him a few times. This fellow in a semi-conscious state and leaning on one elbow in the middle of the pavement said: "Bloody hell do you work in all the pubs in the town?"
Laughs.

Can you think of any local 'characters' you encountered?

There was a character who was a bookie's runner in the days before betting shops. This fellow worked for Keegan Brothers who had a premises somewhere in Quarry Street. They didn't need much room and they just had the one telephone where they took bets and laid them off with a bigger bookie. Jack Turner was a runner. He would spend most of his time in the Market Hotel down Court Street. Punters would come up to him and bet half a crown or whatever on a horse or dog and you would just write it down on a piece of paper. There was no such thing as a betting slip.

Each punter would have their own secret name for identification purposes, which they would add at the bottom of the bet. Unfortunately you could have a couple of hundred old ladies betting on Lester Piggott in the Derby all with the then very popular nom de plume *OXO*.

I'd been on my holidays to Blackpool and there was this chap who was really smartly dressed. He was there with his wife and two kids. He was away a day and I used to see him at nights at the bar and I got talking to him.

I said: "You're a lucky bugger. You're away all day while I'm digging great holes in the sand and you seem to be leading the life of Riley!"

He said: "I'm a race horse owner."

So I told him that I like racing and I found out that he had been at Haydock Park that day.

"I have to go," I said. "What's your horse called?"

"Cockle Kate."

Well I told him that was coincidental. The horse was called Cockle Kate and I was a fishmonger. I told him that I'd like a bet on that and he gave it the thumbs up for Haydock Park the following Saturday.

Well you know how this story's going to go. Anyway I was in the pub on that Saturday afternoon.

"I was on my holidays last week," I said.

"Oh yes."

Not much interest in that.

"I got talking to a racehorse owner."

"Bloody hell. A racehorse owner and you talked to him?"

"Yes."

This certainly got some attention.

"Did you get a tip then?"

"Oh yes. I don't know how good his set up is because it has affiliations with my trade I'm going to have a do!"

"What's it called came the reply?"

"Cockle Kate," the name echoed around the tap room.

Later on Jack Turner walked in.

"Hi Jack," I said. "A five bob each way on Cockle Kate."

"A top pocket bet is that Tom."

"How do you mean a top pocket bet?"

"Well, it's that bloody bad a horse I've no need to hand it in. I'll stand it myself!"

Laughs.

Well you know what the end of the story is? It came last!

The week after when I went in the pub and all I could hear was: "Here he is! Bloody Cockle Kate! What a bloody tip that was!"

Laughs.

When did you finish in the fish trade Tom?

I was in it for thirty years, up to the 1980s. It wasn't the same really when they changed from the old market to the new and the rents accordingly; it was never the same to me. All the heart had gone out of it. So in the 1980s I decided to leave which was quite a change really. I got myself a yard and a couple of wagons and men and opened a scrap yard.

I had a guillotine machine which would cut through anything, I was working on it one morning and it had been raining and it was rough ground which got wet and slippery. I had a horrendous accident with my arm on the machine which nearly took my arm clean off. It was hanging on by a thread. The bloke who was working near me saw what had happened and picked up a piece of waste cable off the ground and made a tourniquet. I was never the same after that. I was off work for ages and it cost me a lot of money, so much that I nearly lost my house. But I have a very good family and eventually after a hell of a struggle I got straight.

Later on I got a job at the brewery, which seemed like everyday my horse had come in! It was a really good job and being a driver I would be out in the wagon around the Ribble Valley and so on. This was my last job and where I retired from.

Did you go to any dance halls?

I went to Tony's Ballroom. It was my main place. A fantastic place that. One of the reasons that I liked Tony's Ballroom[2] was the snack bar they had there. It was during the

---

[2] *Run by Tony Billington*

war and they always had good food, meat pies and stuff that had gone off the market. He must have had some connections somewhere.

Wasn't Tony's a popular place for American servicemen?

The Yanks were based in New Mills Street, up Whalley New Road. You come to a large garage showroom on the right before you start going up Whalley Old Road. They were billeted in the old cotton mill. These were combat engineers and it was the first time that I had seen a bulldozer in real life, or even a black soldier as many of these American's were.

A friend of mine told me this story about an old market man, called Frank Smith, a butcher in his day. At the bottom of Whalley Old Road a railway bridge crosses the road and there was a train full of yanks all leaning out of the carriage windows. The train was stopped at the signals or something.

Frank and his mate were just below the bridge and shouting: "Give us some gum. Have you got any gum?"

So some of the Yanks started chucking stuff down and of course there was a scramble to pick up what they had thrown down. Frank got some chewing gum and a packet of something he said he'd never seen before, being a good Cathol c boy. So he took it home and he put his dad in a very embarrassing position.

"What's this dad? I've never seen this before?" His dad chucked them on the fire!

It's sad that Tony's is closed now but one Saturday I was passing and the door was open, so I thought right I'll have a look in. It had hardly changed. They still had the old settees around the bal room floor.

You couldn't get an alcoholic drink at Tony's so we used to go into the Queens. Mrs. Gregson was the landlady at the time and she must have made a packet out of us and the Yanks.

Tom enjoying a holiday in later life.

Another picture of Tom enjoying a holiday.

Ada Thomas

Born 1927

Where were you born Ada?

In Edith Street which is just off Queens Park Road.

My father, who was called David, was a foreman up at the transport depot. This was Blackburn Transport. He was there when trams were in operation and then when buses took over. It was his job to see that the buses went out and came in on time. He was also in charge of the cleaners. In those days the buses and trams were absolutely spotless!

Did you have any brothers and sisters?

Yes, I had an elder brother and sister and a younger sister. My brother died but my elder sister is eighty six years old and my younger sister is living as well.

Was your mother a housewife or did she go out to work?

She was a housewife. She worked up to me being five years old. Then my sister was born. Up to then my grandmother lived with us. She then went living with her other daughter in

Blackpool. After the birth of my younger sister my mum always stayed at home.

Do you still remember the names of the shops around Edith Street?

I can remember all the shops! There was a corner shop called Hunt's - a mixed business of groceries and confectionary. They actually baked the confectionary on the premises. One of the things that I best remember about this shop is in those days shops didn't seem to sell things like tins of dog food but there were some dog biscuits called Vim's. I can remember the advert, *Dogs Love Vim's*!
Laughter.
Mr Hunt used to have a sack full in his shop doorway which he used to serve from. When we were kids we used to pinch a couple. Not that we could eat them!
Laughter.
I bet you tried one though Ada?
Well, yes, we did try one!
And you've still got a lovely coat!
Laughter.
This was at the corner of Randal Street and Queens Park Road. On the other corner there was a bank of shops. One of the shops was run by two sisters who my mum called *old maids* but I think they were actually widowed or had boyfriends killed in the First World

War. One part of the shop was millinery and the other part was jewellery, but I think they also sold rugs too. I think that the shops are still there, as well as the house that I was born in, number 23 Edith Street.

Edith Street was a cul-de-sac so it didn't go on to Queens Park Road itself. I lived in one of the two top houses.

Across the road on Queens Park Road there were numerous shops. There was a toffee shop called Aspinall's and for some reason we called it *Old Eppies* This was a very old fashioned type of shop with all the sweets in jars and those who ran it seemed very old too.

Can you remember any of the public houses in the area at this time?

From Audley Range right up to Queens Park Hospital there were no pubs whatsoever. I don't know how true it was but my dad always said it was church land. Now I know that the house that lived in was on church land, but he always said that there was something that forbids anyone from building public houses on that land.

What games did you play as a child?

We played Ralivo. I played it on instructions from my elder brother Frank, bearing in mind that anything that Frank said I did. He was seven years older than me and he was my hero. I thought he was wonderful. I had an older sister and she didn't count!

At the back of the house we had this den, which was built around a lamp, the old gas lamps. To light them a man would come along with a pole and he would open the glass and turn the light on. I think they must have had a pilot light.

To go back to Ralivo, we used to have two sides, which were picked by one of us. I always got picked last as I was the smallest. Then one side would hide and the other side would go to find them, catch them and put them in the den. Then one of those that hadn't been captured would try and release the others that had. When he or she saw nobody guarding the den they would dash in and shout *RALIVO*! Those that had been captured would be out again. Now that's how we played it.

I was allowed to play out until 8:00pm. In Blackburn we had a phase where we would be playing marbles. Then it would go on to where may be playing two balls. Then perhaps when it was getting better weather we might play hopscotch. We used to draw an aeroplane shape on the pavement with the numbers on. I never knew what triggered the change of games but suddenly everyone would start a new game. Top and whip was another game we played. We used to chalk a pattern on the top and when it spun round it would be all different colours.

Skipping was another game with the rhyme: "House to let enquire within, when I go out, such and such a body goes in."

We would say their name. Double skipping as well using two skipping ropes was popular and making tents in the back yard. My mother was very good. She would let us use her old sheets for the tent, so we were dead popular and the other kids would come in our back yard. She did lots of baking and she would provide cakes for us to eat in the tent.

My brother Frank was a source of entertainment all his life. He was always the smallest of his age group but always the ringleader. He would think up all these good things.

Frank Higham went on to be leader of the Blackburn with Darwen Council at the time. They amalgamated in the early 1970s. He was leader of the Labour Party and became council leader. We were members of the Labour Party most of our working lives.

He was always in trouble when he was a boy. He got up to all sorts of things. He decided that he'd like a chemistry set which he made fireworks with. I can remember one of the ingredients of the fireworks was iron filings and they made everything sparkle when set alight. After this Frank decided to have a go at making gunpowder.

Laughter.

He did make this gunpowder albeit unknown to his dad! He used to get little bits of silver paper from cigarette packets, and he would put this powder he made in tiny little squares of the silver paper and screw them up. After this he would take them in the back yard and hit them with my dad's lump hammer, to make them explode. Of course all Frank's friends thought that this was brilliant.

Now higher up on Queens Park Road Frank's friend, Jack Wignall, lived. I'm not sure if Jack is still living now but I think he moved from Blackburn. We were both friends with the family. My friend was Jack's sister Eileen. Jack's dad was a builder and he made a big greenhouse in his back yard.

One day Jack asked Frank if he could have some gunpowder so he could have a go with it. Frank agreed and gave him some so Jack took some home. In those days the lads all wore short pants. In his wisdom Jack decided to use the whole lot in one go!

Laughter.

Jack ended up smashing a few flags in his back yard, a few windows broken in the greenhouse, but also these bits of silver paper were stuck to his legs!

Laughter.

His mum was one of the most impressive people I have ever seen when she was angry. I can see her now on her way to our house.

"Where's Frank Higham!" She had a big bust which lurched from side to side.

I dashed into the house and shouted: "Quick Frank hide!"

Laughter.

I thought she was going to kill him!

Laughter.

I can't even remember the outcome but I think that Frank got a belting off my dad for that. By this time mum and dad were a bit fed up with Frank and his chemistry set as he had been making a nuisance of himself all round.

So my mum told my dad that the chemistry set had to go. What do you think she did? She threw it on the fire of course!

Laughter.

You've never seen such a display! Some of it shot up the chimney. Others around the room there was soot all over and my dad's language was choice!

Laughter.

I think that Frank was even in trouble for that as well.

Another thing that the lads did was tie the door knockers together of the houses in the terraced streets. They'd then knock on the doors. When the people went to open their doors they couldn't as the door knocker was tied to the house facing.

Laughter.

I'm glad that doesn't go on now. I wouldn't be happy with that.

Laughter.

There's people who still knock on doors and run away today Ada. They're called Parcelforce.

Laughter.

Most of my childhood was spent in Queens Park in the park itself - right up to leaving school. Even when I finished school and started work, the park was our happy hunting ground!

Laughter.

In the winter we would go sledging although we didn't have a sledge. We couldn't afford one. We used planks of wood, or a tin tray was ideal.

Which school did you attend Ada?

I went to St Joseph's Roman Catholic School in Blackburn. It has been pulled down now. I think there could be a mosque on the site now. They built another St Joseph's Church on Audley Range. My sister Mildred used to attend there but apparently they are short of priests now. Mildred is my elder sister. She used to get upset about the vandalism to the church. It's a sign of the times. What a shame as it is a lovely little church. My mum was buried from there.

At what age did you start school?
I was three when I went to St Joseph's. At that time my mum was working in the mill and my gran was looking after us.

Which mill did your mum work at?
I think that she worked at practically every mill in Blackburn. She loved weaving. She talked about the different mills she worked at but when I was three she went to work at the Alexandra Mill on Mary Street which was just below St Joseph's Church and School. She used to work long hours so I can only remember my grandma being there and not my mum. By the time my mum had come home from work my gran had done everything. My dad used to work nights a lot as well as days so we had to be quiet and my gran was adept at keeping us quiet.
When I was five my younger sister was born and my grandma left to live in Blackpool. I think that there was some bother in the family and she upped and left. I really resented my younger sister thinking she'd been swapped for my grandma. That was in my mind because I can remember disliking her. As soon as my grandma had left my mother was

lumbered with four children to look after. She had help all her life. She had finished in the mill of course.

I don't know what happened before I was born in 1927. This was only just after the General Strike. My father was on strike and he didn't get reinstated to well after I was born. It must have been really tough on the family. They had two children and one on the way and my mother working in the mill. Her mother was living with them so they were probably keeping her as she had no pension.

My mother used to tell the tale that she worked right up to me being born and I was only a fortnight old when she went back to work. I was brought up on a bottle but I can remember vaguely relatives taking babies to the mill for the mothers to breastfeed them. They used to sit outside the mill and breastfeed the child.

When my dad was reinstated in his job I can never remember a time when we had no money although it was hard in those days. I was fortunate. A lot of girls at school had fathers who couldn't get work and it stayed like that until the war started.

Most of the neighbours were in a similar position as ourselves. I wouldn't call it an affluent area just a good working class area where everybody seemed to work. The girls I knew whose parents didn't work generally didn't live in our area. They were from the other side of Audley Range.

Can you still remember the names of the teachers at St. Joseph's?

Yes, I can remember Miss Mercer, Miss Bradley and Miss O'Malley. She was a horror! Being a Catholic school we had nuns in the infants school. It was Sister Ignatius who was always slapping you on the hand and having you sitting next to people that you didn't really like. Our headteacher was a nun. As was Sister Antoinette who taught us. She was only a small woman in stature but a delightful person.

I stayed here until I was fourteen. I took my Eleven Plus and failed. I wasn't clever enough to pass the Town's Scholarship as they called it then. Catholics would go on to the Convent of Notre Dame which was on Whalley New Road and then, I should think, St Mary's College. They had two or three free places for those who only just missed the scholarship with the council. I went to the convent and did the exam and passed it. A little later I got a letter saying I could go to the convent. I took the letter home highly delighted and looking forward to going. There were two other girls also from my school and both of them were only children.

I remember giving the letter to my mum.

She said: "I don't think you can go. We can't afford to pay for the uniform."

You had to buy all the uniform and what have you. I was quite put out about it.

"We'll see what your dad says about it," my mum said.

My dad said: "Oh well. There's no point is there for a girl?"

He was a right intelligent bloke but they concentrated more on lads then, but by this time both Frank and Mildred were working, so I didn't get to go.

When I look back I never really regret it and I'll tell you the reason why and I told it to my friend. When I was eleven these other two girls who also passed this exam to go to the convent were just as clever as I. So I was left but I could beat the entire class now.

Laughter.

If I had gone to the convent I would have been a little fish in a big pool. Now I was leader of the pack.

Tell me about your father.

Dad was in the army during the First World War. There were five brothers and they all came back. That's incredible isn't it? My mother had one brother and he got killed. He was just nineteen years old.

My mother came from Shropshire so my dad joined the Shropshire Light Infantry and he served in Sellonica. He didn't go to France.

What did you do when you left school?

When I left school you could pick and choose jobs in them days. I started at Saxone Shoes in Blackburn and it lasted three days! The shop was where the armed forces recruiting office is now on Church Street. This was in 1941. I absolutely loathed it so I decided I wasn't going back anymore.

I went working for Universal Leather Goods. Everybody called it the handbag factory. The firm did a certain amount of war work. I don't know exactly what but the bloke who owned it was a German Jew called Fritz Wasserman. I didn't stay there too long but I think that he was one of the people that was taken to the Isle of Man for the duration of the war. They did take the Germans there didn't they? I believe he came here to escape the Nazis. The company was on Ordnance Street, which is in the area of Tesco's Hill Street branch in Blackburn.

I used to walk to and from work in those days. It was quite a way when I think about it. The trams were still in operation and I think that my dad, who hadn't yet retired, was a passenger on the last one, which went up

Copy Nook and along Accrington Road to the depot.

I believe you attended church very regularly?

I used to go to church three times a day and I actually loved it. I still like going in a Roman Catholic Church and smelling the incense and taking in the atmosphere. But I think a lot of it was based on the fear of God and not the love of God. When I look back it wasn't a good idea. They were always going on about Mortal Sin and Venial Sin. I mean, they've two levels of sin! I stopped going as I was too idle to get up on a Sunday morning because I used to work Saturday.

Where else did you work?

You've heard of Waring and Gillow - the big furniture firm? They had a factory in London which was bombed out so they set up production at Alexandra Mill in Blackburn. It was a sewing factory. They were making tents, mosquito nets and all that sort of thing. I had a lot of friends working there and they were getting more money than I was so I got a job there. Waring and Gillow were the best firm I ever worked for. They were brilliant, absolutely brilliant. I worked there for the duration of the war.

I can remember when Russia came into the war. I was only a teenager. Normally we worked from 8:00am till 6:30pm. Production was stepped up and I had to work Saturday and Sunday full time to make tents for Russia. They were one man bivouacs made in a white material because they were using them in the snow.

Waring and Gillow were just in this mill for the duration of the war. When the war ended they returned to London.

By the time the war had ended I was eighteen. For anybody who worked during the war, and they were under eighteen, they could choose where to work. Over eighteen you were directed to where you were needed most.

We had been treated really well by Waring and Gillow. We worked hard but we were really appreciated, well paid and we had a good canteen. I can remember the manager calling us *my little girls*. Her name was Mrs Cully. Mrs Cully dealt with all the staff, but the main manager was Mr Bickford. They both came with Waring and Gillow from London.

I had three choices of employment to consider. The first was learning weaving which I wouldn't have touched with a barge pole. The other choice was the Land Army and I didn't see myself in the Land Army as I was a fancy sort who didn't like to get my hands dirty!

Laughter.

The other was Mullards so I went there. For the first few months I was there I hated every minute of it. I absolutely loathed the place but you couldn't leave and they couldn't sack you! The only way out was if you got into a fight. I remember two girls staging a fight in the canteen to deliberately get sacked.

What would happen to an employee if they did get sacked?

They could just get another job. If you wanted to leave you had to go in front of a tribunal. I was constantly going to personnel and saying *I want to leave*! Three times I went in front of this tribunal. The personnel at Mullards was called Miss Keighley. I can remember going to the third tribunal with her. I made a right song and dance about things. I was no shrinking violet! Anything to get out of a day's work!

At the tribunal they were a lot of stuffy old men, deciding what my future was going to be. I remember going down with her in this car.

"You know they're going to turn it down again," she said to me. "You're not going to get your way."

By this time I was getting used to the job anyway so guess what I did?

I walked into this tribunal and they said: "Oh it's you again Miss Higham!" They used to call me Miss Higham.

"Have you anything to say for yourself?"

"Yes! I've decided I like the job now I'll stay!"

Laughter.

I stayed there until I got married and had my first child. Over the years I must have gone back to Mullards about three times.

Blackburn - In Their Own Words

Vincent Gibson

Born 1931

Where were you born Vince?

I was born at 7 Tontine Street in Blackburn. You can't get much more central than that. It was a cottage type property which was gas lit and had a slop stone. I never went upstairs and don't even know what the toilet was like outside.

I started there aged zero and that's where I lived with my grandmother. I only ever had one grandparent. She died when I was about three or four years old. The only way I remember her is a bundle of clothes. She was very small and always wore a shawl and her clothes went down to the ground. She was a mobile pile of clothes.

I lived with my mother and dad in that house. The only details I remember of that is that I slept in the bottom draw of the sideboard. I can remember that as clear as can be. I lived there from birth until I was four years old.

The only toys I can remember playing with were Parkinson's Pills tins, which I used to play with under the table in the middle of the room. I had a cousin who was older than me and who was going to the convent at the time.

I can remember her coming to see us. That's more or less my memories of the house.

I remember we had a gas mantle and a long bracket to reach to control it. I can remember the fireplace being a very old one and the fire itself was quite high up. The main thing I can remember about the place was it was very crammed. The door obviously opened straight onto the street. We had a big cloth hung down from the ceiling to the floor to stop the draft, I suppose, and a little bit of wood at the side. We had no vestibule.

The table was the dominating factor of the room. It quite honestly filled it and it had the knitted covers on the table legs. They were a flaming nuisance! Whenever I wanted to stand up as a kid, they came down when you got hold of them. So that's a very limited memory. It was a dark place and I can remember that it was cold. That's it. I can remember the street vaguely.

Tell me about Tontine Street at this time.

The house that we lived in was a cottage type. It wasn't the standard size of terraced house at all. The row was all cottages. The main building at the end of Tontine Street was of course a building on Shear Brow itself. On the other corner was the Sir John Napier Hotel which is still there. The Tontine Street sign is still on that building. One coincidence this

year was that I came across the Sir John
Napier statue in Trafalgar Square in London[3].
I can remember when my grandma died and
that's the reason why we moved and I
presume that the house was rented.

Were you an only child?

Yes, well picking up on my parents, I know
very little about my parents. My father, Robert
Gibson, came from Preston. I know that. He
had a few brothers and sisters. I do know that
he had a sister that was burnt to death. Now
whether she fell on the fire I don't know. My
father was a great man. He didn't talk about
the past. That cousin that I mentioned that
went to the convent pestered me like mad to
get information out of my dad. But the past
wasn't relevant. He didn't want to know
about the past.

He worked for Jones' Texterities in Blackburn.
They had a few factories but he worked
primarily at the one on Audley Range. He
completed his fifty years service. The
company made components for looms. They
still exist I think and they're down at
Feniscowles now. He got his gold watch for

---

[3] *This would be Sir Charles James Napier
1782-1853. He started his military career in
the Napoleonic Wars.*

fifty years service after he had completed fifty
four years!
Laughs.
He lived to be just short of ninety four. Even
on the day he died I saw him. He was fit and
well at lunchtime and talking about Blackburn
Rovers and current affairs. He was bang up to
date.

**Why do you think that your father never
talked about the past? Was it because he had
some bad memories?**
I don't really know. Now my mother really
did have a hard time. I don't know anything
about her parents. I believe that she was
orphaned when she was quite young. Her
maiden name was Moran. I believe they met
when she was working at St Anne's
preparatory. That's St Anne's down King
Street. I think that she got married when they
were quite young. I probably have the date
somewhere. They were called Robert Aloysius
Gibson and Agnes Gibson.

**I have always associated the name Aloysius
with an Irish background. Was your father
Irish?**
Quite likely. You always associate Preston
with being an Irish Catholic town. My parents
were good Catholics too.

Where did you move from Tontine Street?

We moved to 23 Laxey Road on the Longshaw Estate. The date could be confirmed because we were the first tenants in the house after it was built. It was about 1934 or 1935. There were seventy two houses in the road. I'm always baffled by how the people were selected. I thought that they were all good class people. We didn't have any roughs and scruffs on Laxey Road at all!

The man who lived at number thirty one, he owned a big mill property on Hall Street in Blackburn. He was a soap manufacturer but a lot of his building was used to store food during the war. They made a particular brand of soap powder that was lethal if you breathed it. It always made you sneeze.

Further down the road there was a family called Shorrock and the son went in the navy. They also ran Shorrock's Security which finished up as an international firm. A number of railway men lived on the road too. That is probably because Lower Darwen engine shed was fairly close. It's only a matter of a three quarters of a mile walk. Obviously for most of my young life the men weren't there. They were away in the forces. For example, we lived at 23 Laxey Road. The man at number 21 was in the RAF so he was away all my younger years. The man at number 25 was also in the RAF.

I'll tell you another thing that is right out of character now. The man who lived diagonally opposite to us was a footballer for Blackburn Rovers and he played in the 1928 cup. That's a footballer living in a council house! They had a mad red setter dog. A right hooligan it was. It was out of control most of the time. All the other people were very respectable people. The estate did change dramatically during the latter part of the war when the extension to the road was built. It went from number 72 Laxey Road which I think was the highest number to Manxman Road. Things changed dramatically! It was rough! I can always remember being asked by one of our teachers to make sure one of the lads came to our school. Their house was fumigated once a month, which will give you some idea.

Picking up on characters, at number 75 was a little old lady who wore a shawl every solitary night - seven days a week. She walked from her house with a pint glass and a cover over it, the full length of Laxey Road up Park Lee Road which was an unmade road at that time, to the Stop and Rest pub on Brandy House Brow. She would get a pint of beer for her husband and came all the way back. Mary Anne we used to call her.

There was another character who I won't name but he is still around and is very public orientated. He looks after the people down Bank Top. He was a great character. The incident I can remember concerning him happened one winter. We were walking in the middle of the road as there was snow covering the pavements. There were about five or six of us and suddenly he disappeared! There was a manhole cover missing! I remember him working as a bus conductor for Blackburn Corporation. When all the kids came out of school they used to look for his bus. Two buses would come. His bus would be full to overflowing. The other one would be empty! I don't think he charged them! *Laughs.*

What school did you go to Vince?
I went to St Mary's Dean Street. I can remember two headteachers. There was Mr Standen who was the headmaster of the boys section but he died actually before I moved into his section. Then there was Mr Turner, the headmaster, who in my estimate, he was a very poor quality teacher.
I started at St Mary's in the infant class. Moved up into the big boys and left at the age of fourteen. St Mary's and Dean Street have now been demolished but the legacy is now the school on Bennington Street, which is still

called St Mary's. I think they moved there in the 1950s.

I wasn't impressed with school. I was impressed with the infant's class because I remember being taken more or less on the first day and they had furniture which was the same size as we were! They were grand chairs to sit on, and we used to have a nap after lunch every day.

There were two nuns in the school, one round the infants section and one round the girls section.

Can you recall their names?

I can't no. I wasn't clever at school - no way! I wrote down my qualifications somewhere. The outcome of my school days were nil qualifications. Talk about me sitting examinations. We never had homework.

Did you sit your Eleven Plus?

I think the school did but I may be wrong here as I don't remember sitting it. I wonder if some people were selected out of the process. It may or may not be correct. I got swimming certificates. I had a wooden reading lamp as evidence that I went to the woodworking classes. That was more or less the outcome of my education, which is minimal.

Can you remember any of the priests from your school days?

Yes, Canon Bousfield. The church was at the top of Dean Street. He celebrated fifty years as a priest so having a Golden Jubilee was a big event in the church. I can't think who took over after Canon Bousfield.

As you would expect, being a Roman Catholic school, it was very church oriented. We went to Mass on a Sunday. You were expected to go to 9:00am Mass. You went in the benches in your classroom. Your teachers were in charge of each section, including one who came from Accrington, I don't know how he managed on a Sunday with the buses.

During the war years teachers would be called up to serve their country. Do you remember any teachers who had to leave?

Teachers were selected obviously but I wasn't interested. Mr Standen then Mr Turner was the next headmaster. He was getting on a bit but he did own a car that was something very unusual. WH5913, I can remember the number of that! He always used to park it against a big air raid shelter, which was built in Dean Street.

Can you remember the war starting and the effect on your family?

I can remember the day the war started as clear as can be. It was a Sunday. War was declared on a Sunday. Our routine on a Sunday was very clear. I went to 9:00am Mass as usual. We came back and had breakfast. The next thing that was unusual was we went in the sitting room in Laxey Road and they had the radio switched on at 11:00am for the Prime Minister's broadcast. I can remember my mother crying and that was my memory of the day war was declared.

I was looking forward to the following day. I didn't tell anybody this as it was one of my secrets! But I was looking forward to drawing the curtains back on Monday and seeing lots of dead Germans because I wanted their helmets.

Laughs.

I was bitterly disappointed when they hadn't arrived and been killed! So that is a personal thing about that particular day. I can also remember the day war in Europe ended. I can't remember what day it was. I feel it was a Friday.

A lad came running into the school and shouted: "War is over! War is over!"

I thought that was quite important news!

With that Mr Turner told him to: "Sit down and get on with your work!"

So that was the beginning and the end of that period.

Can you remember seeing the German aircraft coming over to bomb?

Yes, we were in Belper Street Baths on one occasion and by shear chance we saw a plane going over quite low. There was very little information published then but at the end of Laxey Road there was an anti-aircraft gun and a barrage balloon.

Talking to the crew, you know what they say? Walls have ears, and careless talk costs lives!

We did talk to the man on the anti-aircraft gun and he said that they were there to protect the fuse factory. They also said that the aircraft that came over was looking for the fuse factory. I have a book that has an aerial photograph taken from a German plane over Blackburn and you can see Laxey Road, Park Lee Road, the hospital and everything.

We were extremely envious of the lad who lived at number 33 Laxey Road. His name was Ronnie Connolly. He was blind and went to a blind school in Liverpool. We were envious of Ronnie because he used to come home with shrapnel. We used to swap things for shrapnel but he had an advantage over us as he was more involved than we were.

Did your family have an air raid shelter?
I have some photographs somewhere. Everybody had an air raid shelter on Laxey Road.

Was this at the bottom of your garden?
It was quite close to the garden actually. We used to go in it, plus the two ladies whose husbands were away in the RAF. I have a photograph from after the war. We dug the air raid shelter up and my dad made a shed out of it, so there's a photograph in its original shape and you can see the soil line. I have another photo when my dad shaped it and made quite a nice job of it.

You knew when they were German planes coming over by the tone of the engine which was totally different to ours. We did very well. We didn't have much trouble at all. I found out since the war that a bomb fell on Bennington Street. That's where the new St Mary's school's gone. Obviously the one in Ainsworth Street was well known. There was one in Mellor. We heard those things but we'd no idea where they were until many years later quite honestly.

My dad did two nights a week fire watching duties so he didn't come home during those nights.

Do you remember the Home Guard in the town?

Not really. The only way we came up against was the army. On King Street, next to Canterbury Street, there was an army barracks there. Of course we saw the activity there.

When I worked on Bolton Road there was the Royal West Kent's Regiment stationed at Nova Scotia Mill. The Bren Gun carriers and all them sort of things were running around the town. We used to get planes coming over I presume going to Barrow in Furness and Liverpool and places like that but we never saw much bombing here. The war ended in May 1945. I left school in July 1945 but the war in Japan was still on so the war was still in existence when I started work.

Where did you start work?

I went to work for Sellers the Fruit Sellers, which was the local multiple grocers. Their mini shop was next to the Savoy Cinema on Bolton Road. That row of shops is still there. In fact Bolton Road from the Wainwright Bridge - every solitary building is intact. I know more or less every solitary shop there.

Yesterday I called in at the shop where I started work and its fifty nine years since I walked out of that shop to do my National Service, so I thought I'd call in and see them! I didn't know what sort of reaction I'd get because it's a hairdressers and beauticians now.

Anyway I went in and I said: "I'm not a customer so you're not going to get any money but the last time I walked through that door was fifty nine years ago!"

The lady was elated.

"Thank goodness to meet somebody who knows this place! We've tried everybody but nobody seems to know anything about it!"

I spent about one hour there talking.

I told the lady about life in the grocer's shop aged fourteen. The last job at night was to go into the Savoy Cinema and get the cat because he used to go in there as it was warm. I'd be going down one aisle and the cinema attendant would go down another calling for the cat to come while people were watching the film!

The Lady said: "That's amazing because we have a black and white cat. We have to go to the pound shop further down the road because it goes in there!"

Anyhow, I left school at fourteen and started work at Sellers the Fruit Sellers. I was the only male in the shop between ten and fourteen employees - depending on what day it was.

Was the firm a wholesaler?
No, they were retail with eight branches in Blackburn. They had a warehouse at the top of Kay Street, where Jepson's Mill used to be. Later on he finished up with ten shops in Blackburn.

Who owned the business?
Fred Sellers and he lived on Buncer Lane next door to the Sacred Heart church. He used to drive a Jaguar car w th the letters SS on the front which was rather antisocial during the war!

Laughs.

Jaguar of course had dropped their symbol on the front of the car. I could probably remember the registration number as well!

The van that they had was probably built for carrying dresses. To get in you went round the back of it and opened the door at the back. It was quite tall with all hanging rails inside. That wasn't particularly helpful for us moving groceries!

It was a very good company in actual fact. All the food was loose. Your Danish butter came in one hundredweight tubs whilst New Zealand butter was in fifty six pound boxes. If you happened to get dates, they were in eighty pound boxes. There were cheeses which we used to role down the passage at the side of the shop. They were between sixty and eighty pound. When Greenwoods delivered the flour we had two big bins. One was for self-raising and one for plain flour - in two hundred and forty pound sacks! They used to tip them in. You can imagine all the flour floating around. Sugar came in two hundred weight sacks mainly. A side story there, the sacks were made of good quality jute. When the Ministry of Food or whatever they were called in those days were putting stuff into warehouses, like on Hall Street in Blackburn, you could steal sugar very easily with a pencil. You just put it in and the sugar would flow out.

Food rationing was the corner stone. When a person came to shop they would put their books on the counter.

They'd then say: "My rations please."

This was usually the opening statement.

Then they would ask: "Is there anything under the counter?"

Which there usually was!

I have a lot of memories of that. It was also interesting that the men started coming back from the war. That was interesting because as I mentioned the shop had all females. As the men came home they came to the shop. They were aghast quite honestly at the rations and things of that nature. Then they went to the shop where they were worked before the war and the women got sacked. Very diplomatic!

Of our customers the one that was best known was Arnold Jepson who was one of the owners of Jepson's warehouse. He won the Military Cross.

A character was a man called Dick Washington. He weighed about twenty stone and was a night watchman for the corporation. He sat in one of those huts that looked like a sentry box with the old brazier outside. To let him in the shop we had a split door half opened.

He used to open the door and shout: "Let us in!"

Then we had to go and pull the bolts down and open the whole door. Inside we had one chair for customers to sit down. We called it the *Pan Shine chair* as it had the Pan Shine cleaning agent name on it, but he couldn't get in that, so we used to bring out the three legged stool. We had a twenty stone man sitting on a three legged stool!

Putting his rations on the counter was an embarrassment you know: Two ounces of butter, four ounces of margarine. It didn't relate. The manageress of the shop used to make special provisions so that we could take some food to where he lived. It was totally inadequate that sort of thing.

I used to get our groceries on the Friday night. They had a system. You had to be registered there of course. That was one thing at that time. You knew who your customers were.

The bulk of our customers were weavers. We were surrounded by streets. They shopped twice a day. When they were coming home from the mill at lunchtime, they would come in for what they were going to have for their lunch. They'd buy one OXO cube and five woodbines. Those were the quantities they bought.

They'd then ask: "Had anything come in?"

That was one reason why they called. If they had a family, say of six, they would shop six days a week and bring in one ration book a day to get in the shop and to be aware of anything that was coming in. That was part of the strategy.

What did you do with things that were scarce?

That was a big problem. Staff got a privilege. We could ask for things that came in. I can always remember Scribbans Cakes when they started being made and everybody was after them. I would get a packet of those more a less once a week. I was able to get things for the two neighbours we had whose husbands were in the RAF. They never asked what it was. I just used to select a number of things and pay for them and they used to buy them from me.

Did the shop sell alcohol?
No, no! That didn't come into my life in retailing until some years later and it was a serious problem.

I worked at Sellers until 1949 when I was called up for National Service in the RAF. I went to Padgate first where they made you welcome on the first day. I think everybody remembers their first day. You went in. You went past the guard and you're told to go to a particular hut where you are seated in nice easy chairs. This is all an illusion you know? Then an officer came in and welcomed us.

"You are now in the Royal Air Force and what a good job you are going to do," he told us.

He went out.

"Lets have you outside!" the corporal came in and shouted.

You then went for a knife, fork and spoon and a pint pot. Things like that. The essentials of life! Then they burg you all together again and get you marching and swinging your arms. Of course you break the pint pots and you have to march over to the NAAFI to buy another one!

Then they tell you that there's just about enough time to have inoculations before lunch and you go up steps to a wood hut.

Very dramatic you know? There are two people there and you're told to roll up your sleeves so they can do two arms at the same time. It's all drama.

Then I went to Bridgnorth in Shropshire for two months. The highlight of that was getting out on a thirty six hour pass to Birmingham. I paid sixpence and stayed in a Salvation Army hostel just to get out of the camp. I went to RAF St Athan for trade training. Then the final base was RAF Syston in Nottinghamshire which was a flight training school. They trained me to be a flight mechanic when I was a grocer of course.

I moved to RAF Syston which is near Newark on Trent in Nottinghamshire and had a very good experience there as the commanding officer was keen on sport and I was a keen cyclist.

You must always read the notice board. I arrived at that station on the Monday and got in trouble right away. There were three of us. We'd travelled from South Wales to Nottingham but I knew London. The railway pass we got gave us the route so I said its better, to the other two, if we go to London. We ditched our kit and had a day in London. What we didn't know was that on the last bus to RAF Syston was the station Warrant Officer! He's the disciplinarian of course. I suppose our conduct wasn't the best, for the following morning we had to report to the station Warrant Officer. We didn't half get a dressing down as far as that was concerned. That was on a Tuesday. On the Wednesday I reported to the Engineering Officer as I was working in his section.

The same day there was a notice on the notice board for me to go and see the Commanding Officer. I had to present myself at the Group Captain's office at 11:00am. I had no comprehension what was going on around me.

"What will this be about?" I said to the Engineering Officer.

"I've no idea," he said.

All I can think of was the problem with the station Warrant Officer. Anyway I went. It was the archetypal office. A great big one which I had to march across then salute. The opening statement killed me.

"I see you was fifty fifth in the cross country running down at St Athan," he said.

Well I was stunned I couldn't connect with him you know? I wondered what on earth is this about?

"I see you were fifty fifth in the cross country run," he repeated.

Well I was still putting my thoughts together.

"How many were in the race?" he went on.

"At least three hundred and fifty" I replied.

"Well that's not too bad then. I see you're a cyclist?"

"Yes sir!"

"Have you brought your bike?"

"No."

So he turned round to the Warrant Officer.

"Give this man a thirty six hour pass and see that he gets home to get his bike."

Of course I didn't know that he was an enthusiast also. I didn't know that on the same station was one of the best racing cyclists in the British Isles, Ken Russell, who won the first tour of Britain.

So I represented the station. We used to go to Cranwell for training. I used to fly fairly frequently as ballast in the plane. This was the Harvard tandem seating arrangement. So you could sit in either seat it didn't make any difference.

I was at the scene of the world's greatest air disaster[4].

We were out on the Sunday and there was a Tudor IV coming in and it just dropped. Two ran out. I thought I saw three. The papers said two. It was a Sunday afternoon and it was still daylight. There was a clock at 3:50pm, I

---

[4] *This was the greatest air disaster to date when an Avro 689 Tudor V flying from Dublin crashed at Llandow aerodrome in South Wales 1950. Eighty people perished.*

remember the rectangular shape clock in the cabin. We were there all night so you can imagine the mess. We were there until the Monday morning. It was about 11:00am on Monday morning before we were released and went back to camp.

The aircraft didn't catch fire?

No, it didn't that was the marvelous thing about it. It was just squashed flat[5]. There was a Dakota behind it, a part of the same trip to the rugby match but that landed safely. The Tudor had a poor record. The conclusion was that possibly the pilot's seat had jumped backwards. I don't know more than that.

I had an experience. The only problem I ever had with an aeroplane was my first flight. I happened to be in the front cockpit. It didn't make any difference with the Harvard. We'd gone up over a priory and only just gone past it.

The officer spoke to me and said: "Is there a control column in your cockpit airman?"

I can remember him saying that very clearly.

"Yes sir."

"Well take the plane up to three thousand feet and fly straight and level."

---

[5] *The aircraft may have stalled on landing and dropped to the ground, turning over in its descent.*

I was sweating but I knew about the theory of flying as I had been in one of them rig things. So I did that.

"Ok I'll take over now," he said.

We did the air test. We were testing the aeroplanes, giving them one thousand hour flight checks. We used to go out and do the air test often doing the stall and then just came back it was as simple as that.

When we came back the officer spoke to me.

"Right, we've got a problem on our hands. We'll have to do the necessary documentation."

The control column had come out in his hand! It was one tube going in another with spring loaded lugs and it mustn't have been shoved in far enough. There was a court martial but I didn't have anything to do with that. It obviously happened during the aeroplane's servicing!

After that all the flights that I went on were no problem whatsoever. It amazed me the instruction you used to get, the flight instructions. You had a pad on your knee and you would wear a silk overall. I think that was so you didn't hook on things.

The instruction would say:

Fly and turn left. Fly to Newark on Trent.
Turn left up the A1.

Theses were the flight instructions!

Do a 180 degree turn and come back.

But the last line was always the same.

In case of fog land at the nearest clear airfield.

That was extremely helpful!

I once got caught out. Course you get to know the test pilots. We had a Wing Commander in charge. I saw him as an old man yet he was probably in his late thirties. I don't know but that was how I visualised him. He was a big man as well. He told me what he would do and flew straight back.

"The test is now complete," he'd said.

I let my straps off. But then he started doing aerobatics! I crashed my head on the top! Do you know how in comics you see the characters seeing stars when they bang their heads? Well I did see stars! So that was a lesson learnt.

Basically the National Service experience was good.

Can we return to your childhood Vince? Can you remember any shops or chippies from those days?

Yes, I'll go back to before I started work. The route from our house on Laxey Road to school is indelibly imprinted in my mind. Once a week I used to meet my dad coming home from work on Friday lunchtime. We used to call in the shop at the top of Infirmary Street. There was a sweet shop there. I used to get barley sugar twists on a Friday when my father was bringing his wage home.

Continue to the junction of Mosley Street and Infirmary Street. There's a Primitive Methodist church on one corner which has just recently been knocked down and the man who owned it lives down the road there. There was a butcher's shop on the opposite side of Infirmary Street. There was a grocer's but I can't remember the name now. I used to go in there for a Harrison's loaf - sliced and fresh. They were the instructions I got from my mother. I had the money wrapped up in newspaper.

On the other corner there was a clogger's shop. Actually a school mate of mine went to work there. Further down Mosley Street was a Dewhurst & Johnson. This was a multiple grocers where we used to shop for our rations. We would go in once a week.

There was a big Coop on the start of Mosley Street; I worked for the Coop for thirty odd years so I know that one well. There was a plumber's shop near Hall Street and Mosley Street and I could never understand why there was always a roll of lead outside the shop about seven or eight feet long.

Even in those days people would say: "That lead is very valuable."

And I would wonder why people didn't steal it?

Of course you couldn't even move it!

Hall Street and Mosley Street: On the other corner there was a wallpaper shop, and then there was a chemist at the far end was the clogger's shop.

Mosley Street had a dip in it which is still there, there was haircressers shop there. The notable thing about that was the lady who ran it. She had big boobs!

Laughs.

Must be the reason I still remember that!

Across the road was a confectioners and one of my friends lived next door to that. They were gas lit.

Can you tell me the name of the barber you went to?

I can remember that it's on Mosley Street and is now a chemist.

The next barber I went to was on Bolton Road, there's a kink in Bolton Road. It's demolished now and is the B&Q site. That was where I went but I can't remember his name.

How old were you when you came out of the air force and returned to Laxey Road?

I was twenty.

Did you go to any of the dance halls in Blackburn at this time?
Never!
I was a trainspotter as a kid and Dean Street opened up onto Islington and the railway lines. I collected train numbers. Something that was very relevant in the war time. One day I got a massive surprise. It was a miserable February. A train came out of the mist with a totally different silhouette than I had ever seen before. The right hand side was the United States Transportation Corps. It was an American locomotive that had been shipped into the Clyde and was working its way South for the invasion. So trainspotting was the big thing! This was in 1943.

So dancing was not an interest?
No, nor girls. They hadn't been invented!
Trainspotting was the big thing as far as I was concerned. To get from different places I got a bike. Over a period of five or six years I changed from being a trainspotter to being a keen cyclist. So that's what happened.
Another thing that I saw was the Coronation carriages. They were stored at Lostock Hall and were blue and silver. We used to go round Horwich engine railway works. You couldn't get a permit to go round as individual kids so we used to walk around the

outside to see what we could see. We noticed on a Saturday that respectable looking people walked down the works drive.

"With the party?" the man on the gate would say.

"Yes," they'd reply.

"Just go down there the second door on your left there'll be tea and coffee and the guide will turn up."

So they were being conducted round the works. So my best friend and me got dressed up and left our bikes out of site. We got through the gate using the same answer to the gate man's question. We got a free visit round the works.

Then I changed over to cycling which kept me occupied and that's how I met my wife. We were both cyclists.

We cycled everywhere, including almost the full length of the Pyrenees in 1954. That was a long train journey. We set off at Saturday lunch time and it was Monday lunchtime when we got down to Toulouse. Then we cycled in an easterly direction and joined the Pyrenees and came right back to Biarritz on the Bay of Biscay.

Do you still cycle?
No. We packed it in, probably about 1960.

Where did you work?
From 1945 to1949 I worked for Sellers the Fruit Sellers.

From 1949 to 1951 I did National Service.

From 1951 to 1984 I worked for Blackburn Coop.

I Started in the grocery department of the Coop and worked in about thirty different branches. I started as a sales assistant. Then first assistant. Then manager at four or five shops. I then won a scholarship, a very valuable scholarship, and went to the Coop College down in London. Everything was paid for plus 2/3 of pay as well. That was the first time I got rich!

Then I became a shops inspector, personnel manager, and then did a lot of secondments for the CWS in Manchester. I did one or two odd jobs. I was the chairman of the North East Lancashire Distributive Training Group. I was the National Treasurer of the Cooperative Personnel Services Association.

Not bad going for a lad who left school without any qualifications.

Well I had no qualifications. I deputised for Jack Straw once. He had a job here and there was a three line whip in parliament and he couldn't come. I met King George VI twice on a casual basis and President Mitterrand. I met the Duke of Southerland about three years

ago. I know the Duke of Rutland's dog but I don't know him!
Laughs.
The meeting with King George VI was so simple really. My cousin's husband was a Warrant Officer in the Royal Artillery based in St John's Wood in London. King George VI was keen on horses and he used to go there regularly. I stayed at their flat in St John's Wood and one morning I went into the stables. I was looking around the stables and this man came along. We said good morning and we exchanged a few words. Then he went on his way.
"Did you see the king this morning?" my cousin's husband said when I returned.
"I thought I recognised his face!" I said!
Of course I was probably only thirteen or fourteen at the time. I didn't go to the pictures much so I didn't see the news reels. I met him again later on.

Can you tell me something about the famous Coop divi?
It depended where you were. In Blackburn it was always a piece of paper with your number handwritten on. Every six months it was all toted up and you could go and get your dividend which was divided according to how much your purchases were.

There was an individual shop in Blackburn, Blackburn Excelsior shop on Lambeth Street. They had tokens and had forty thousand registered members! That was incredible. The Coop is a nineteenth century invention and really it shouldn't exist in this monolithic joint stock company world but it does!

It comes out great with this shambles we have with banks at the moment. The Coop bank is like a shining example of a well run business. In fact I used to occasionally lecture at Blackburn College. The head of department asked me to do a talk once for their business studies HND people on the *History and Organisation of the Cooperative Movement.* There's just not much in text books quite honestly.

You mentioned Darwen. I worked for the Coop later on and they had a shoe shop on the main road which we took over sometime in the 1960s.

There was a door and I said: "What's behind this?"

The reply was: "I don't know we haven't been upstairs"

I went round to the office for the key. When I went up the stairs there was a complete shoe repairer's workshop from before the war. All the boxes, all the labels, all the tools, everything.

The Coop Museum in Manchester came and took the whole stuff out.

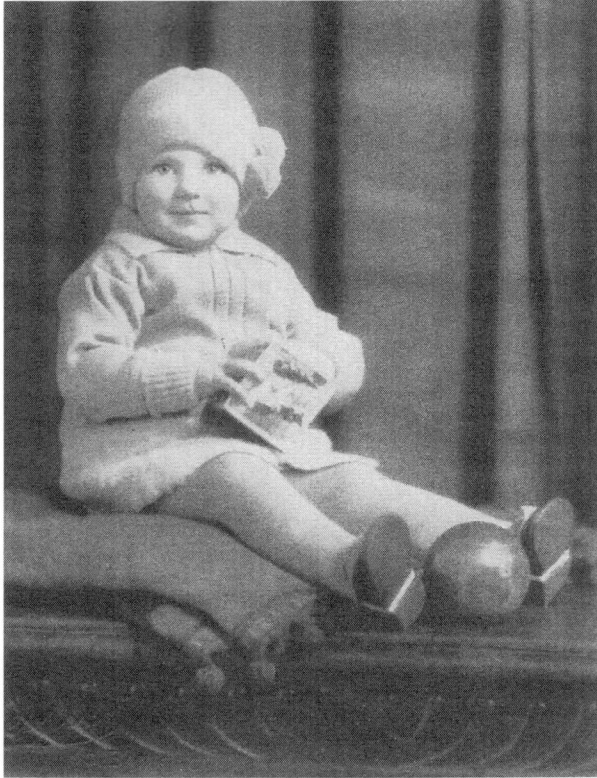

Vince Gibson as a toddler.

Vince Gibson is pictured third from the left in the centre row. Photograph taken August 1949.

Vince's parents pictured in their garden at
Laxey Road.

Bill Entwistle

Born 1922

Tell me about where you lived as a child.
We first lived in Turton Village. Then later on we moved into one of three cottages that belonged to New Eagley Mill. They were tied cottages belonging to the mill as my father worked for them. There were three cottages altogether. We lived in number three. It was comical when the war broke out. They built air raid shelters for one and two as they came under Bolton Council. We were under Turton and District so we didn't get the shelter!

Did you go to the village school Bill?
Yes I did. It was called Bank Top. There were never more than ninety pupils there at one time. The school had four teachers. The headteacher was Miss Abbott. She gave me an interest in nature and poetry which I'm still keen on. Miss Abbott was absolutely brilliant. When I was thirteen, the year before I left school, a trip was organised to Windsor. My parents had four kids at home and they just couldn't afford for me to go, so she insisted on paying. So I went to Windsor and saw the

castle. The next time I went there, when I was older, was to guard it!

I can remember all the teachers at Bank Top. Miss Ainsworth took the younger ones. Miss Simpson took the next lot. Then there was Miss Walkden. Just four teachers who were there throughout my time at the school.

Is Bank Top School still there?

No it's not. They pulled it down and built another at the back of it. Tony Knowles the snooker player bought the current property where the school once stood.

When I was nine years old I started taking milk round. I took the milk round the village until I left school. The milk was put into cans and I would empty the milk into the jugs on the doorstep, morning and night. If I spilled a drop of milk on the doorstep I was in trouble!

What was your father's occupation at the mill?

He drove a steam wagon. I can tell some tales about that! He was fined for speeding once! He was going fourteen miles an hour when the speed limit was twelve.

Laughter.

He got fined five shillings.

The boundary that separated the two councils was the river. That must have been altered.

Once, a man hung himself from the bridge over the river. My dad called the police and they came.

"It's not ours it's Bolton's!" they said!

They stood arguing about who should cut him down!

Laughter.

So you led a very rural life in your boyhood days?

Yes, very. It was a mile to the nearest bus. I worked in the cotton mill for five years, spinning with a 90% humidity. I used to work barefooted. There was no such thing as health and safety then.

I then volunteered for the Grenadier Guards and did three and a half years with them. I went to Chelsea Barracks, originally to Surrey, but the main training was done at Windsor.

How did you take to army life?

I really enjoyed it I did eighteen months at Windsor. It was the perfect place for troops. It had the river, the Great Park and the castle. It was a garrison town and they were used to troops. Every few weeks I would be on guard at the castle, a forty eight hour guard. I had a great time there. I joined as a regular soldier but in 1942 I was sent out to join the battalion which was in Egypt. We went all the way up the desert with the Eighth Army. One of our main battles was the Battle of Mareth Line in North Africa in 1943. That was one of the fiercest battles we fought in the Second World War.

I was a member of Number One Company and was one of the lucky ones to be rescued by the Bren Carriers. Only four of the six carriers returned safely. Basically we were surrounded as we went too far. Two of the Bren Carriers were blown up. One of the Bren Carriers blown up had my platoon officer and the company commander on it. The Platoon Officer was Mark Bonham Carter. He got taken prisoner. Funnily enough, just before I was wounded Lieutenant Bonham Carter escaped from a prison camp in Italy.

A fortnight after the battle of Mareth, where a lot of people had been killed and just buried in shallow graves, we went back and dug them up, reburied them and gave them a religious service. Then a stone cross was erected later where the fighting finished. Some of the graves were also moved and the cross was brought back to England and placed facing the guard's chapel.

When I was wounded Lieutenant Bonham Carter immediately wrote to my parents.

In the letter he said: "I am unable to do anything here, but I will ask my mother to write to you."

His mother was Lady Violet Bonham Carter. She actually wrote to my mother.

It was a really genuine letter saying: *If your son comes home and is in the South of England, don't bother about accommodation I will put him up.*

When I got back to England I was in a hospital in Cheshire where I stayed for six months.

I believe there are six of us left that fought in that battle. I've been to a few reunions. The last one I went to was two years ago. I was introduced to the Duke of Edinburgh. I've been introduced to him twice. I was introduced as a survivor of the Mareth Battle. I have also been to Buckingham Palace garden parties four times now and also met Princess Anne. I've got about a bit!

Laughter.

The first time that I met the Duke I was introduced as somebody who was with the Eighth Army.

He said: "Oh, there was a lot of Grenadiers in the Eighth Army weren't there?"

I said: "No. There was only one battalion and not many of them left."

"Are you sure?"

"Of course I'm sure!"

"Why are you so sure?"

"Because I was there and you weren't!"

Laughter.

And we got arguing!

A friend of mine came over and said: "You're quite safe I'm his minder."

Laughter.

The Duke was great with me. His final words were: "Where do you come from?"

"Lancashire," I said.

"Oh!" he said!

Laughter.

The Duke spoke to the organiser later and said how much he enjoyed the argument.

Laughter.

I stopped going to the reunions at one point but in 2000 I joined again. I was in Portugal and I went into a restaurant at the hotel one night. I saw a bloke with the regimental tie on. Well I had a regimental tie too so just for a joke I went behind him and tapped him on the shoulder.

"Why don't you get a decent tie instead of that thing!" I said.

Well we got talking and kept in touch and he made me a member of his branch in Nottingham. He was younger than me and in the regiment in the fifties. He died a couple of years ago.

We had a sergeant in our battalion who was also called Entwistle. He was a big tough character and an army boxing champion. He was a pre-war soldier. Whenever we used to bump into one another we would put our fists up and have a playful scuffle. I didn't see him until I moved to Blackburn in 1960. I went to do a job at Blackburn Police Station, and who was there but Sergeant Entwistle who was now a police inspector. Immediately we started a scuffle!

"Hang on Cyril if anybody comes they're not going to ask any questions!" I said.

Laughter.

Cyril lived in Lower Darwen and later moved to Australia. He died two or three years ago.

In 1961 we lived in Bromley Cross. After the army I joined the Post Office as an engineer. It was the only job I could get as I was one hundred percent disabled.

I was a bit bitter when I left the army. I was in hospital for ten months after I was wounded and was in various hospitals in Naples, Tunis and Algiers, the hospital ship and finally Cheshire.

I was discharged from the army in August 1944 when I was still in hospital. I remained there until September 1944. When I was discharged I lost my army pay and became a civilian! I got two pounds a week pension from the army, and out of it I had to pay the hospital for my keep. There was no health service in 1944.

That was a terrible way to treat someone who put their life on the line for their country.

If they would have kept me on until I was discharged from hospital I would have been alright.

This is unbelievably callous.

I actually had to pay for my keep in hospital. I was very bitter about that.

Can you tell me the extent of your wounds Bill?

In the chest, a piece of shrapnel went through my lung and liver also taking a rib out. They gave me the shrapnel they took out. They told me afterwards that I walked four miles to get treatment down a mountain.

The medical treatment I got was unbelievable really. I went to a casualty clearing station which was basically a tent. The medical treatment that I got was unbelievable. The nurses there were working twenty four hours a day, but they still found time to write to my parents.

I was wounded on the 9th November 1943 and was discharged from the army on the 7th August 1944. I was in a civilian hospital in Cheshire which had a military wing and I came out of there in the middle of September 1944.

I went back home, but having had this sort of injury to my chest I didn't want to go back to working in a cotton mill.

I didn't have long convalescing as I had to get a job which I did for the Post Office, climbing telegraph poles, after ten months in hospital.
Looking back on it, it was the best thing I could have done. It helped me to rebuild and that's what I needed. I finished up staying for thirty eight years. I was based in Bolton originally. Then I moved to Blackburn. Then Burnley. With a bit of studying and hard work I got to a managerial position.

Tell me about your married life.
My wife came from Bolton. Both her father and brother worked for the post office as engineers. I was married for forty eight years. My wife had Parkinson's disease and passed away in 1993. I had a heart attack in 1991 which I was told was due to the shear stress of caring for my wife. When I came out of hospital I was told that I wasn't fit to look after my wife and she went in a home.

Did you go shopping in Blackburn in your youth?
I remember when the market was built. I put telephones in there. I avoid Blackburn if I can now. I do the shopping at Sommerfield's in Clitheroe it's much easier to get to on the bypass. I also like to shop in Booths.

What were your hobbies as a young man?

I used to do a bit of dancing in the local dance hall, and went to the cinema. I didn't go dancing much in Blackburn. It was mainly at the Bolton Palais. Everybody used to go there at least one night a week.

I played quite a lot of cricket. I played for the Whalley second team for a while and I was captain for seven years. This was in the late 1960s and early 1970s. I played a lot of badminton too. I ran the classes at the Harrison Institute in Blackburn for fifteen years. I got paid well for it too! When I had the heart attack I had to give it up. I used to really enjoy it. I first started playing as a kid at the village school. I also played at a club in Ribchester.

What games did you play as I child?

There was no football pitch, only the school yard so we played football and cricket. We were allowed to play there after school. There was a tennis club in the village so we never ran short of balls to play with.

I would go to the cinema too on Belmont Road in Bolton. It was called The Bell. I remember seeing my first talkie there. It was called Disraeli. I used to go the Saturday afternoon matinée.

I never went away when I was a kid. The Bolton holidays were the last week in June and the local farmer did his haymaking then. My dad always used to go haymaking. That was his holiday and we went as well. All the hay was put in a big barn and pressed down to get more in. As kids we got a few coppers for jumping on the hay.

Did the local farmer take on Irish labourers for the haymaking?

No. He wouldn't have them as he had had problems with them in the past. The farm was Bank Top Farm which was run by Harry Abbott. My mother's step sister married Harry, who was a local character. He had a brother who had a farm known as The Oaks which was near the railway station. When Harry was ready for the haymaking, me and my brother would go up to The Oaks for the horse which Harry used to borrow.

Did you encounter many Evacuees?

While I was away my mother took an evacuee from Guernsey. Her name was Edna Ruth Carrick. When I got home there was no room for her, and we didn't get on very well. She was a bit flighty. She was about fourteen or fifteen at the time and was sent to live with someone in the Manchester area.

97

Tell me about your time in the army.

When I went abroad we went on convoy on the Atlantic bound for Egypt on a former London to New Zealand meat ship. We were lucky. We never got attacked or saw a thing. There were thirty six from our regiment going to join the battalion and we were made the ship's police and given an arm band each. The cells were all air conditioned so at night we would turf the prisoners out and we slept in the cells. Two of the prisoners were Glasgow blokes who tried to murder a corporal on the ship. There were some rough characters. One of these Glasgow lads showed me how to hold a razor when you slash somebody. Glasgow red skins they were called. They had a civilian trial in Durban I believe.

On New Year's Eve there was a dance on the top deck of the ship for officers, warrant officers and ATS girls. There was a hundred of them on. Just imagine what the troops thought about that! The dance had been on for about thirty minutes then the police were sent for. We got to the top deck in time to see the piano being thrown overboard!

One night a friend told me that he had met a girl and she knew me. This was in Slough. He said that she'd like to meet me again. I knew her. She came from Bolton. She had been moved to work in the Labour Exchange in Slough and was billeted with a family in Slough.

The family was a chap and his wife and their daughter. They had a fish and chip shop. So I went to see her and started going with the daughter!

Laughter.

I wrote to her all the time I was abroad. They were a Welsh family evacuated to Slough before the war. I saw her when I came home. Then when I was in the hospital in Cheshire the consultant came to me one day.

"I've got to tell you it's unlikely you will be able to work again," he said.

So I wrote to her and broke it off. There was no future for her. It was sad really because two years after she died. They were a smashing family. I can see the father now. He was a big Welsh chap. My pal and me would go to the door

"Come in troops!" he'd say.

With having a chip shop he always made sure that we had something to eat.

I still have her photograph.

The Guards Chapel in London was struck by a flying bomb in June 1944 on a Sunday morning during church parade. Many

Guardsmen were killed[6]. Every June they have a memorial service. They call it Black Sunday. I've been down to it. I mean to land right on the Guards Chapel. It has since been completely rebuilt.

There was a Congregational Chapel in Turton village called Bank Top Chapel. It may have had a name changed to The United Reformed Church now. In the chapel a plaque was erected in the memory of two local lads who died in the war. One of them was Bert Holden, who was about the same age as me. He was in the RAF and he was killed during a bombing raid on Tripoli, North Africa. Now I was in Tripoli that night and I remember the raid. I didn't know that Bert was there. He was a member of the ground staff.

We stayed in Amet. I was in the Battle of Amet during the war and the Battle of Tunis. On holiday in Tunisia this German chap decided to tag along with my wife and I and two girls who kept being pestered by the Arabs.
One night this German said to me: "Don't you speak any German?"

---

[6] *On June 18th 1944 121 military and civilians were killed and 141 were injured.*

I said: "Only the bit I learned from the prisoners I took during the war!"
Laughter.
He never spoke to me again.
Laughter.

I go away on holiday with a Jewish friend who was born in Belgium and came over here in 1936 because the family could see what was happening. Her grandparents stayed over there. About six or seven years ago I went with her and her sister to Antwerp and we found a school that they went to and the house where their grandparents once lived. The house was taken and the grandparents disappeared and they don't know what happened to them.
It's funny they went to this house in Antwerp.
The nephew's wife said: "Lets knock on the door and see if they'll let us in!"
So she knocked on the door and a big black girl came to the door.
Diane said to her: "Do you speak English?"
She said: "Yes. I come from Birmingham!" in a broad Brum accent.
Laughter.
She invited us in.
The house had been turned into flats and they were now on the ground floor where the kitchen once was, with the same tiles as they remembered them as kids. They found the

school that they went to as well. She's now eighty three years old.

In the war she joined the WAFFS and after the war she applied for a job in Manchester.

She was told: "I'm sorry. It's company policy not to employ Jewish people"

She had just come out of the WAFFS! She was a bit bitter about that.

That's terrible Bill, really disgraceful

Yes. They'd never get away with that now.

I was in the Home Guard in Bolton and that was comical. I was only a teenager when I joined the branch at Astley Bridge. The local butcher was the captain and the mill owner was involved. We had to do nights even though we were working the next day.

Did the unit have any live ammunition?

I had my own gun, a 2.2 Winchester Repeater, from when I went shooting rabbits. We lived on rabbit meat during the war. It was difficult getting ammunition for the gun. The only way I could get the bullets was by going to Bradshaw Police Station. This was on the understanding that I had to lend them the gun occasionally!

Laughter.

Before the Home Guard it was called the LDV or Look, Duck and Vanish.

Laughter.

Did you have a uniform Bill?

No, just an arm band. did about two years in the Home Guard then went into the army.

During the war, on guard duty at night, we wore gym shoes so we didn't make a noise as we were outside apartments. Both the Royal Family and the Crown Jewels were at Windsor during the war.

There would be two of us on duty of a night, one with a rifle and bayonet and the other with a Tommy gun. There was one bloke called Hubert Collet. He was six foot four and a massive build. One night we heard somebody coming as in the black out you couldn't see much. turned out to be the inspector in charge of the castle police.

Hubert said: "Wait until he comes past you Bill and I'll challenge him and you come behind with the rifle and bayonet."

He challenged the inspector holding the Tommy gun.

"Halt who goes there!" he shouted.

But he couldn't remember the password! We kept him there for two hours!

Collet was six foot four and I stood behind him with a bayonet. He was frightened to death!

Laughter.

Hubert was a pre-war soldier and was to be taken prisoner at Dunkirk and put in a POW camp in Luxemburg. He escaped. He worked his way across France and Spain. Then he pinched a rowing boat and rowed on to Gibraltar where they arrested him as he had no identification you see.

Collet was a real character.

When he was interrogated he said: "I'm fed up with this. Who's in charge of this bloody Island!"

Laughter.

He was told it was Lord Gort who was a Guard's officer before the war.

Hubert said: "Then bring Lord Gort. He knows me!"

Laughter.

So they decided then that Hubert was who he said he was. He was awarded the Military Medal for escaping like he did.

I saw Hubert after the war then I lost touch.

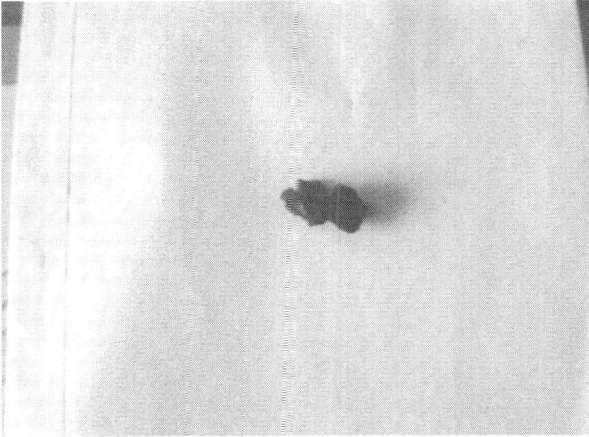

The piece of shrapnel that went through Bill's lung and liver.

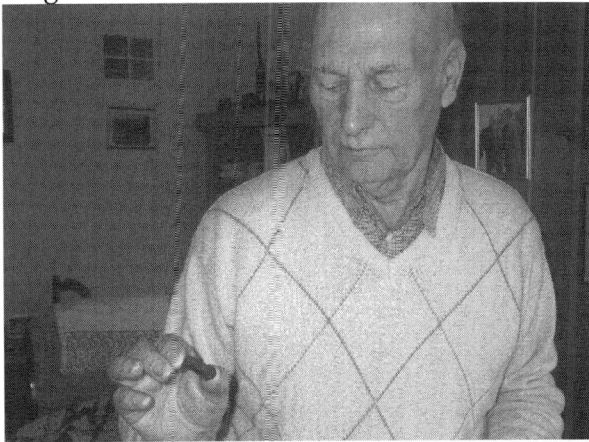

Bill holds the piece of shrapnel that nearly ended his life.

Howard Talbot

Born 1941

Howard I'd like to go back a few years and talk about your dad, Wally Talbot, who like yourself, was a well known local and national photographer.

My dad was born in 1914 and he started work at the Telegraph in 1928. The job that he started on was given the title *the devil's runner*.

He started there when he left school at fourteen. He went to the Parish Higher Grade. That was the old school in those buildings that are now used as offices at the cathedral. The school later moved from there to St Peter's where I went at Byrom Street. It's no longer there now.

The editor at the time my dad started was a bloke called Cuthbert. I think that was his last name.

"There you are," they said as they handed my dad a camera.

"What's this?" my dad said.

"It's a camera! Just go out and take photographs."

Was your dad interested in photography at the time?

I can't remember but I don't think so. Not when he left school.

Perhaps your grandfather then?

Well my granddad started Talbot's Funeral Service on Whalley New Road. It's now positioned facing the cemetery. My granddad started that with his brother. What happened there was unfortunate.

"Have you ever thought about selling your business?" this guy said to my granddad's brother.

Taking it as a joke he mentioned either a thousand or two thousand quid. I'm not sure which. This was probably in the 1920s. I'm not sure.

Anyhow this bloke said to my granddad's brother: "Stay there."

He went somewhere and got the money and sorted him out.

He came back and said: "Right the business is mine now!"

His name might have been Bentley. I know a Bentley owned it later.

My granddad didn't know that his brother had flogged the lot and that was it.

My granddad went on to start up Blackburn Carriage Company, which was on Weir Street. This was another funeral business. He started with Belgium Black horses, two to a carriage and he had about eight horses in all. My dad used to drive the horses as a lad.

When I first went to St Peter's, when I was eleven, having left Roe Lee School, I used to get the bus around the park at Roe Lee Park where I lived at number 85 and it took me to town. I used to walk past Weir Street sometimes and see my granddad. I can remember him being at his desk in the window, one of these big sloping desks. I used to nip in and say hello and then I'd be off to school. This would be about 1953.

What was your granddad's name Howard?

Charles Henry Talbot. His brother was called Thomas. My granddad lived up at York Crescent in Wilpshire. I remember as a nipper going around there in a little pedal car. I pedalled from Roe Lee to see my grandma and granddad and forgot to tell my mum where I was going. I was only four or five and she went absolutely berserk!

Tell me about your photography.

Safety didn't come into it in those days. The health and safety lads would have a field day today!

My dad would climb up chimneys, Blackpool Tower, Winter Hill. We both did to get a good picture. What good would a safety hat be falling from a chimney anyhow?

Laughter.

I've no idea!

I got swung in a bucket when I did some work for Brooke Bond in Manchester. We used to do Brooke Bond food in Great Harwood and Manchester. I went up in this bucket on a crane about two hundred feet up to photograph some silos they had put in so they said that I had better wear this safety hat.

"Is that going to do me any good if I fall out at two hundred feet up?" I said.

"No, but the health and safety bloke's watching!" they said.

Laughter.

So I got into this bucket with this guy. We had to wait until the bucket had stopped swinging before I could get some photographs and then I had to lean over. As I did this my hat kept coming off. I finished up taking it off and putting it in the bucket as I thought that if it fell off it could land on somebody.

Yes. Probably the safety officer!

Laughter.

Tell me more about you father, Wally Talbot.

My dad worked for the Telegraph up to the war. Then he was a photographer during the war for Bomber Command 150 Squadron. He got mentioned in dispatches and received medals and whatever. He flew on bombing raids and helped compile maps. I have a big book of photographs that he took.

The poor lad was dying of cancer and one day he just wanted something to occupy his time and thoughts.

"What can I do Howard?" he said to me.

"Why don't you put some captions to the book? You've told me about them many times - but if I go nobody will know what they are."

So he started to type some captions of what was in the book so in later years when people look at it all the information will be there to see. That's what he did until he passed away. He was ill for twelve months then that was it. My dad came back from the war in 1945 or 1946 then he rejoined the Telegraph.

Who owns the copyright on photographs?

At the time when my dad worked for the Telegraph, the paper held the copyright for the photograph but you could hold onto the negatives. In 1988 this changed to whoever took the photograph held the copyright as well.

Did he take many photographs of celebrities?

Before the last war the Telegraph rang my dad up one weekend to tell him to get a photograph of Charlie Chaplin who was playing in Blackburn. My dad tried to track him down but he had gone out of the area and not many people managed to get away from the old fella!

He photographed Ghandi down in Darwen. They used the photograph that he took in the Ghandi film. It was taken outside of Greenfield Mill. This was in 1930, two years after my dad started with the Telegraph. He stayed with the Telegraph until 1952 or '53. Then he had a bit of a bust up with them.

He was always giving photographs away was my dad. He would go to Ewood Park when Rovers were training or whatever and take a number of photographs. He would always get a few prints made and give them to the players. There was never any charge as many times the players would be willing to be photographed in their own time. He was told that he would have to charge for the prints.

There were other things too probably so he decided he'd had enough and went working on his own. He started doing weddings and portraits and even went knocking on doors to build up his business. He started getting work with newspapers and then that grew. I joined him in 1957 straight from school and it was all newspaper stuff.

I photographed Bobby Charlton a number of times. Bobby Charlton was all right with us. You had to coax him. We did hear reports where he didn't want to know but we found him fine. My dad photographed him very

early on, in about 1961, for the FA Book for
Boys where they used to do features on
players. There would be a lad who won a
competition to meet h s favourite player and
we did quite a few. Bobby Charlton, Jimmy
Armfield and Ron Clayton were some of the
players. My dad would go along and the lads
would be in their football strip and have their
photographs taken with their heroes.

Matt Busby's son, Sandy, rang me up two or
three years ago as I had a photograph of
Sandy when he played at Rovers. I took a
picture of him running around the pitch on a
training day. He was with Ron or Doug or one
of the lads. He had seen this and found out
that it was my picture so he rang me. He lived
in Manchester and he wanted a couple of
pictures for his grandchildren.

I photographed PJ Prooy at King George's Hall
in a velvet suit and later I had a beer with
him. He was good and kept coming to the
front of the stage going down on his knees. I
thoroughly enjoyed that night.

My dad photographed Paul Robeson and
Johnnie Ray.

George Formby was photographed in Africa
during the war by my dad. George was there
entertaining the troops.

My dad had an exhibition after he'd done fifty
years as a photographer and it was held in the

museum. I kept the photographs and the library has them now in their vaults.

You mentioned your dad being unlucky in tracking Charlie Chaplin. Did you find that celebrities in years gone by were more willing to have themselves photographed for the publicity?

The Charlie Chaplin story was a case of not being in the right place at the right time because I'm sure that the lad himself wouldn't have minded. They didn't in those days. Hardly anybody would not want their photograph taking. In fact it went the other way. They wanted to be photographed because they wanted to be top.

Nowadays you can get in all sorts of trouble. We used to do a bit of that too! We took photographs where we shouldn't have done. We would stand at a front door and take photographs with the subject in the room.

Would this be for the local paper?

No, by 1958 we were doing a lot of work for the national papers. If we got anything it was a bonus for us because when the newspapers used the photographs you would get a publication.

In those days there used to be about six publications. Papers such as The News Chronicle, The Daily Sketch, The Mirror,

Daily Mail and so on. We used to drive to Manchester to all those places.

How many photos would you take at an average football match?

Well you really had to read the game as far as goals were concerned as you only had one chance. There was always the chance that the ball would hit the post and someone else would bang it in. Ther you'd lose it.

My dad devised a method using a grub screw and two 5x4 cameras. The cameras were screwed together so that you had one at the top and one at the bottom, so you had another chance if you missed the goal first time.

Then we got quicker cameras. We went from 5x4s to the 2¼ Roloflex where you could press the trigger then wind on, so we screwed those together too.

After that came the 35 mils with motorised Nikons. With those you just pressed your button and off it would go. Nowadays it has gone way beyond this. Way beyond. You don't have to do any focus or light judging. None of this. I wish it was like that for us. We used to do weddings and if that went wrong you couldn't do that again.

In the winter when we covered the football we were using deep plate cameras then glass plates and film 5x4s. You would hold the camera and sometimes it was so cold that you couldn't feel your hands. You hopefully pressed the trigger and prayed it would work. You couldn't feel the trigger!

Were your football photographs published regularly?

We used to do all the football pre-season press days. We would get a head and shoulders photograph of the players, not necessarily in a team group. Most of them you did but Manchester United wouldn't. The only team group we ever got of United was in 1974 when Tommy Docherty was there and when they won the European Cup in 1968. We used to do this up to 1991 - every player.

We used to go to the Rovers, Burnley both Manchester clubs, Everton, Liverpool, Leeds, Bolton and others. We'd photograph every player every year.

These would appear in the papers, in special pre-season editions, and say for instance George Best scored for United, the paper would use the photograph we had taken along with the story. We would get paid for that. Our details were on the back of every photograph that we took. We made six prints of every player for the nationals to use.

How did you usually come by your information regarding breaking news?

We would get tip offs from the taxi lads, police, the fire brigade, whatever. Sometimes we'd get there and the police would be arriving.

"How have you got here?" they'd say.

"Well we were just passing!" we'd say.

"Oh yeah!"

It was a living if we got in first and got six orders from newspapers. We would get three guineas for an ordered job but you could be on it all day, just for three guineas. Not much money for a full day and then you had to go into Manchester. We would get mileage allowances and allowances for the materials.

The guy who did the Brewery Street murder[7], King, used to be brought in from Risley in the Black Maria. Then they had to back the

---

[7] *The Brewery Street Siege took place on the 12th/13th of December 1958. Estranged husband Henry King, twenty seven, held his wife, Sheila, and her family at gunpoint. Sheila was shot dead during the ordeal. Two policemen, Chief Inspector O'Donnell and DC James Covill, were also shot during the ordeal. Sadly, Inspector O'Donnell died later in hospital. King was found guilty of manslaughter rather than murder due to diminished responsibility.*

vehicle down through the cobbled street to the charge office to get him into there. We would try to beat the dailies because they were always around when that happened because of the high profile nature of the case. Then there was the widow and the funeral and all the people involved. It all went on for some time. Then they had to bring the accused back every seven days to be remanded or else he was a free man.

I was speaking to the police. They used to call me Tich then as I was only a kid. My dad was bigger than me. They always called me Tich. They still do!

"Can we not get a picture of him coming out the back?" I said to this bobby.

"No, we're supposed to keep him covered up," the bobby said.

Anyway, me and my dad hid in King George's Hall toilets downstairs. I was stood on the loo looking out of the window and my dad was down below with the windows open and I had the top window.

The accused was brought out to be put back in the Black Maria. There was this policeman. The accused was cuffed to him. He saw us did this guy and he put his hand up to cover his face.

When I spoke to the policeman afterwards he said: "What were you doing?"

"We were taking photographs," I said.

"Why didn't you let me know? I would have kept him down!"

The photographs were passed on to the six dailies.

We got him a couple of times. I borrowed a *Long Tom* from the Telegraph, which was a camera that my dad used for the cricket and scenes around Whalley and the Ribble Valley. It had a telephoto lens.

We were in the garage which was next to the mortuary at the bottom of the police yard on Northgate. We borrowed my granddad's blanket which he always used for covering his car up. He nursed it, polished it and always covered it up at night. I weren't too popular as I cut a hole in it and put the camera through.

They used to arrive at the charge office with him at about 8:30am, We would have been there since 8:00am. t was in the middle of winter, dark and very cold. In those days the yard was blocked off at the bottom and the Black Maria would back down the yard. The van would stop and the police would get out with him and bang! Get it home, get it developed and off to the dailies.

We did that a few t mes and this one time I was talking to this off cer.

"What do you want Howie?" he said. He always called me Howie.

"All the bloody press are here. We're never going to get anything!"

119

"Have you been to school lately?"

"Been to school? What you on about?"

"Have you been to school?" he again repeated. "Did you go to Blakey Moor School Howie? I suggest you should go!"

"Oh right! Ok!"

So I told the old fella what the officer had said and he couldn't believe it.

"You're joking!" he said.

"If we get in that school yard they're gong to bring him through so that he doesn't go out of the charge office or anywhere near the other press lads who are awaiting at the top of the hill."

So me and the old fella went into Blakey Moor School yard. The door opens and out he comes down the steps. He was cuffed and he put his hand up to cover his face which was good for us because he couldn't be identified. We got him and beat all the other lads. They couldn't believe it!

What kind of work did you do for the nationals?

My first day duties with a national paper were with the Daily Sketch. I couldn't drive as I was only fifteen or sixteen so I had to go on the train. I used to take 5x4 cameras and films and slides in a bag and I'd do a day duty.

They'd get me around by taxis to do my jobs. Then I'd get on the train for home at about 6:00am. Other times I would have to do night duties and be there for about 6:00pm and work through until about 2:00am.

I would go on different jobs throughout the night. Sometimes it would be a road traffic incident or fire or even a murder, whatever came in.

My dad was working for the Daily Mail. One time my dad went up to the photographic department up in the main dark room and there was this guy and he had a big bin. He had these glass negatives and he was smashing them on the corner of a desk and throwing them in this bin.

"What are you doing?" my dad said.

"I'm getting rid of these. They're taking up too much space."

"Leave them," my dad said, "I'll sort them out."

"Right, right, I'll leave you to it then."

There were copies of prints from the 1928 Rovers Cup Final against Huddersfield Town. All sorts and this fella was destroying them!

My dad brought them back and I have them now. There's photos of Harry Healless walking around Wembley with the cup and coming back home on the coach. It was ironic really that when the team were due back in 1928 from Wembley, my granddad offered to pick the team up and drive them, but they wouldn't let him because of the crowds and the safety issue.

How did you train to become a photographer?

I used to mess around with cameras in the studio before I left school because we moved from Roe Lee to Preston New Road. I used to lark about with the cameras and the old fella was always coming in with his stuff.

At Roe Lee, when my dad first started on his own, the dark room was my bedroom. My dad would black the window out and he would print at night time. He did weddings, commercials and so on and I used to sit on the edge of my bed whilst he would throw about six sheets of paper that he'd exposed in the dish. I used to print them, put them in the wash then put them in the fixer. That's how I started learning.

When we moved to Preston New Road I used to help my dad quite a lot and pick up a camera and start larking about with it. When I left school I had no job to go to other than working with my dad.

There was a guy called Sharples who used to teach photography at the college of a night time. My dad suggested that I go along to see if I could pick anything up. I went and it was mainly theory and that didn't interest me one bit. I just couldn't get into it at all. I kept writing all this about convex lens, concave lens and all the other technical jargon and this just didn't register until we started taking photographs of people. I was learning more on the job through my dad, what to do and what not to do. So I packed it in after going a few times. It just didn't interest me at all.

During the war the old fella went to Cranwell for his learning. He had to pass tests at Cranwell and just scraped by on the theory tests. He said he was hopeless at it yet my dad had been using a camera for years! On the practical it was easy though. He had to go and photograph say a bomber, inside outside, front, back and the panels, on the cockpit too, everything. I've still got the photos. They're in his book.

Did your dad become an officer Howard?

A sergeant - 981734. I even know his number!

Laughter.

I remember him telling me that all the other lads who came to the RAF straight from university struggled with the practical tests but were good on the theory. Most of them hadn't a clue! They were asking him *how do you do this or how does this work?* Not a clue.

A picture should tell a story. When we did a picture for the nationals it didn't need a caption. If a bloke rescued a kid from the canal you'd take the bloke and the kid to the canal, and get a picture of the canal, the kid and the bloke. If they didn't use the photograph you didn't get paid.

Did you ever do any writing?
My dad was good. We would get through by writing captions for the photographs, and you had to dress your captions up. We first started when we got a picture of a goal. You know Chinagraph Pencils? You would get a ruler and draw arrows indicating the path of the ball in either red or black Chinaraph. Well we started that and when it went to the nationals they would wipe the Chinagraph off and replace it with broken lines or dots on the finished newspaper pictures. Once we had started doing this everybody else started following suit.

The Mirror would send photos that we took all over the world. People were clambering for pictures all over the world. The National Enquirer would pay us three or four times more than the nationals would pay us if they used our pictures. The pictures we sent to The Mirror were syndicated until we found out and we didn't get anything from it. If a picture was reused we should have been paid but we didn't get anything and these pictures were being published all over the world.

We did a lot of football pictures for the annuals Charles Buchan and so on. My dad did Ron Clayton and Jimmy Armfield. You would do a picture of Ron in his newspaper shop with his wife and then out delivering papers and a story round it a feature - or we'd do one on Tom Finney in his overalls as a plumber.

Tom Finney was a smashing fella to deal with. He was a wonderful fella. I photographed him a few years ago at Preston's football museum. Tom had a do for this unveiling of the beautiful life size bronze statue of himself.

We got Tom, Nat Lofthouse, Bryan Douglas and Ron Clayton behind it. As were the Preston and the Blackpool lads. Johnny Haynes was with the ads too and sadly died a couple of months after the event had taken place.

The old fella told me off. I did some pictures of Tom once during the week and we processed them and my dad told me that they were not good enough and that I'd have to do them again! So we rang him up and I went back on the Sunday morning. Tom was fully kitted out and I did some more.

I had one of the ground staff throw a ball for Tom off camera and Tom leaped up for the ball. I did the pictures in colour and in black and white and I still have them. Tom gave up his own time on a Sunday morning. You wouldn't get that sort of cooperation now, unless you had an open cheque book for an agent!

Laughter.

Stanley Matthews was red hot. My dad got on well with him. He photographed him right from an early age. When Stan got his CBE my dad photographed him and I went with him to Stan's house in Blackpool. I still have the negatives.

There were various reports that Stan Matthews was a bit standoffish.

Yes, he was a bit as you say standoffish but if you showed him the colour of the money he would do it. He was a bugger for that was Stan.

Laughter.

I have some signed photographs that he did for my dad. They say *Wally, all the best Stan.*

My dad always got on well with him. He got on well with all of them. But a lot of it's down to how you work them. If you're abrupt then they'll just close up. You won't get anywhere.

When the pictures were done we'd give them a load of prints which they thought was great as fans would often come to them and ask for a signed photo so it worked both ways: Give and take. When you went along the next time you were in! You had your foot in the door.

I wouldn't like to have to do it today. Everything is done through agents. I've noticed nowadays in the paper that the only pictures you see are the lads running or kicking a ball about. We didn't want that. That sort of thing was old hat to us. You had to get them doing something. We got Burnley's Jimmy Mac as he was playing golf and placed his golf ball up a tree then took a picture of him scratching his head as if to say *how do I play this shot?* That's what the newspapers wanted, comic stuff.

I remember old Jimmy Milne, manager at Preston, he used to have a pole with a rope attached so that players could run and jump up and head the ball.

I wanted something different and Jimmy said: "Get them heading the ball."

I thought *if I go back with that my dad will play bloody hell!* I had to wait until he got out of the way to get them to do something else. I got the players on a tractor and grass cutter. The inference was that *we are going to cut the opposition to shreds on Saturday*. You really had to use your imagination to get something different and all six newspapers would use it.

I remember we did one of Ally McLeod. When they were training they trained on a place next to the ground called Little Wembley. It was all cinders. If you fell on that you'd rip yourselves to shreds. I used to play with them. If somebody shot the ball from one end there was no nets so the ball would go straight into the River Darwen, so someone had to go in for it.

One particular day in the middle of winter the ball went in the river and Ally was going to get it.

Me and my dad said: "Ally just do us a picture will you?"

"What do you want now Wally?" he complained. He was always complaining but he liked the attention.

We took a picture of him in the River Darwen which of course wasn't deep where they were as they could walk just in. We got him to kneel down! So there Ally was up to his knees in water and he was laughing his head off. Then he picked the ball up. We told him to hold the ball up then we photographed him.

When we got back to the studio my dad said: "We could do with some snow."

So what he did was use this stuff called opaque which when you blotted it on a negative it will come out white. So my dad brushed it on Ally's shoulders and training kit top together with some white blobs on his hair. He was just training for a cup match but dressed up it went in all the newspapers.

It was sometimes a hard game to be in. For instance, when a story broke we had to hang around to try and get a picture. Sometimes you would be there for hours so you got used to missing meals. The reporters were alright. They could go off to the pub and work on a story but not us. No picture no pay.

In those days we used to cover right up to Blackpool as freelance photographers. Not to mention all East Lancashire right down to Colne and beyond. There weren't many freelancers then.

Covering football matches you really had to wrap yourself up. You got some bad weather, sleet, snow and rain. An old mate of mine, a policeman, one of the old borough lads, gave me his cape, which I had to take the buttons and numbers off. If you weren't a policeman you weren't allowed to use it. I got stopped many a time at grounds by a policeman asking me how I got hold of the cape. I used to say that there's nothing on it so it doesn't matter. They'd say ok and leave it at that. What I used to do was sit on a box and pull the cape right round me and have the cameras underneath. I'd have a hat on of course too. The cape did the trick. I never got wet with that around me. It was ideal because when you sat down it came down to the ground.

When the Rovers went down they weren't as popular with the newspapers but my dad always had a contract with The Sunday Express to do Rovers one week and Burnley the next. There was still an interest but not a top interest, like when Tottenham or Man United played. I got a contract in 1968 with The Sunday People. The guy who used to be the sports editor there was from Darwen, Harry Peterson. Harry asked me would I do pictures for him. This entailed me doing Man United one week and Man City the other. This contract took me from 1968 until 1980. I saw some fantastic games. Now that was football: George Best, Denis Law, Charlton and Francis Lee!

There was a photographer on the Munich trip who I knew. He helped pull the survivors out of the plane with United players Harry Gregg and Bill Foulkes. His name was Peter Howard.

I recently did a book for Bill Foulkes, not a full book but it features some of my pictures. He got in touch with me. There's one picture I took at Blackburn and a group picture of the 1968 European Cup team.

My dad was working for The Daily Express on the night that they printed the programme with no Man United names on it. This was the first game after Munich in 1958. United were playing at home and my dad photographed the team coming out to play Sheffield Wednesday. Albert Quixall was playing for Wednesday and he came to United that same year.

Did you ever do any celebrity or sports personality weddings?

Yes. Jimmy Robson did his wedding, Roy Vernon's and Keith Newton's wedding.

Weddings are a different kettle of fish, one off days. We used to go early to photograph the bride, the groom and the best man.

There used to be a church on Preston New Road and I went there one time and asked for the best man and the groom. Nobody knew where they were! I thought *right, where's the nearest boozer!* There was one down the back of Preston New Road. I thought *that's the nearest* so I went in.

"Aye Howard how are you alright? Come on have a pint with us."

"You're supposed to be at the church! I've had to send the bride away and told her to go round again. She turned up and there was nobody there! I had to ask one of the taxi lads to drive her round the block while I went to find you. Come on, let's go!"

"Oh we'll just have another then we'll be there."

Anyway reluctantly I managed to drag them out of the pub.

"Look there's a back way into the church. Go in the back way."

"We're not going in the back way. We're going in the front way!"

Then the groom spotted the taxi with the bride in it and went over and knocked on the window.

"How are you love? Are you alright?"

I thought my goodness me that's a good start. He's starting the way he means to go on!

Laughter.

My dad was on one wedding at Mellor. They were all in the church and it came to when the bride and groom were exchanging vows. Will you take this woman and so on.

"No!" the groom said.

"Excuse me but I don't think you've heard me quite right," said the vicar. "I shall say it again."

So the vicar repeated the vow and the groom again said no and turned around and walked back down the aisle. My dad and the best man went running after him but it was too late. The groom headed for the fields over a wall and off! Naturally there was all hell to play, but someone managed to get the groom and bring him back to the church. Of course the bride and all her family were very happy about all this! Eventually though the groom went through with his vows. How long the marriage lasted, don't ask me!

I remember when my dad chased The Beatles. He was over in Blackpool and he ran through this field. He didn't know it at the time but it was a sewage works! What he was doing there I've no idea.

Perhaps that day he didn't feel like work and he was just going through the motions. Laughter.

When he got home he absolutely stank to high heaven. In the house at Preston New Road, downstairs we had big stone sink, the same size as a bath but square. We got it from Shaw's at Darwen to wash all the photographs in. My eldest sister dumped my dad in it and his clothes and she scrubbed him!

He got an infection in his hands and they swelled up to twice the size. They were like Andy Pandy hands. He could hardly get his hands into the camera with this swelling.

My dad went to see old Doctor Driscall who had a surgery on Birley Street up Whalley New Road. When he came back his face was ashen.

"Are you alright? " my mother asked. "What's happened? What did he do?"

"He just looked at them and saw how they were - then got a pair of scissors and stuck them in and popped the swelling."

The old fella nearly keeled when he did this. He was always in it my dad!

Laughter.

So that was all through chasing the Beatles?

How he ended up there we still don't know to this day.

I photographed The Beatles at Preston Guild Hall. The fans went berserk. I think that the lad's favourite sweet was barley sugar. The fans were throwing these from all over the hall onto the stage which was covered with barley sugar. They hurt too when they hit you! I was just in front of the stage so as well as being pelted on the head and back by sweets I got knocked all over the place by the fans who kept moving forward.

Did you talk to any of The Beatles?

Only backstage before they came on. I didn't have a great deal of time. I was in and then out. There were a lot of photographers there that night so it was just a question of getting the pictures as quickly as I could. These pictures went in The Mirror or Mail. I can't remember now.

On a Thursday we used to go to Blackpool for an afternoon out but we would be partly working anyway. We would take my mum and the rest of the family. This would be in the 1960s and '70s.

We used to do the bathing competitions because there could be Miss Great Britain or

Miss England. Generally when we photographed the winner of the competition there would be a well known star posing along side of her. Edmund Hockridge, Morecambe and Wise, Bob Monkhouse and Tommy Cooper. Stars that were appearing at Blackpool for the season. They'd go along to help judge the competition so you would get a picture with the star holding the girl or pretending to throw her in the sea.

The next day the picture would be in The Daily Mirror so in other words you got paid for going out with the family! The stars loved it. They would do anything for the publicity. Get them to wear different hats or lark about. They would do anything! So this paid for the day out.

I used to do a lot of work for the Mecca Organisation; I photographed Frankie Vaughan, The Dallas Boys and Tony Christie.

My dad was a best mate of Harry O'Hare. He was another old Telegraph lad who was a processor with the Telegraph. He was a funny lad. He passed away a couple of years ago.

Harry had a pub at Whalley and Barrow and once had The Feilding's Arms. No matter where you saw him in town he always had a joke for you, always a joke. You could never get a word in edgeways!

In the dark room he had a big wooden table and Harry used to dance on it having leapt up from the floor. He would tap dance there! *Laughter.*

He was absolutely brilliant! What a character. Smashing fella.

Laughter.

That's something that you never hear now Howard. Nobody ever tells a joke. Even on the television comics don't tell gags the humour is so different now - don't you think?

I don't think they're funny! All our family were always jokers. My Uncle Les, when we had family dos, was always a joker and pulling your leg.

We didn't go out much. My dad had just come back from the war and Saturday nights were always at Uncle Les's. He lived at the top of Bold Street off Shear Brow and on a Saturday night we would have pie and peas with pickled onions and have a good laugh. We would play records and mime to them. I was only a lad then and I had to do a character called Nellie Lutcher, who was an old black American singer. At the time we lived in a council house in Roe Lee Park. It was a smashing place. It still is.

At Christmas and on birthdays there was always a do. We made our own fun. My sister used to tap dance and I would be dressed up like Nellie Lutcher with my mum's old head

scarf and I would mime to her record *Come on Down to My House Baby.*
We are going back a bit Howard!
Laughter.
Just a bit. I were only a lad then.
Laughter.
The last comedians to make me laugh were people like Frank Carson and the lads from The Comedians, Jimmy Tarbuck and Freddie Starr.

I used to do all the Wilpshire Golf Club photographs, which they always wanted in sepia. Then one year they asked for a change so I did them in colour, so I started the first colour photographs at Wilpshire. Then we did Blackburn. Pleasington always wanted theirs in black and white. Eventually they changed to colour.

Did you ever do any ghost stories?
Not really as such but at Samlesbury Hall I can remember we used to take wedding photographs and I used one of the rooms that was said to be haunted by the White Lady. The room was full of stuffed animals. It was ideal for me to go up the stairs to this room and take pictures of the wedding party out of the window of the guests down below. I could get them no matter where they stood. My dad

came up the stairs after me one time.
Unknown to me he locked the door.
Laughs.
"Come on aren't you coming down?" he
shouted from down below. He knew that I
couldn't as he had locked me in. The room
used to frighten me to death. It gave me the
collywobbles!

Talking about ghosts, this is a true one which
involved my son. Now if you ask him about
ghosts he'll turn white at the thought of it! He
had a proper experience when he went to stay
at the home of one of his mates in Batley in
Yorkshire. They owned this old hall.

This guy was in the weaving business and
he'd talked about ghosts with his mate.
Anyhow, he went and stayed there. One night
in the room which he stayed in he saw this
apparition. Everything went icy cold and he
went cold too but started sweating.

He saw this vision which came through the
bottom of his bed straight through the bed and
along. He ran to his mate's room and flew
through the door. The pyjamas that the lad
had on were wet through with sweat.

What was the subject of the apparition?
It was a person walking through the room and
he was told that there was a ghost that walked
along what used to be the landing.
"Are you pulling my leg," I said to my son.
"Did you have a few beers?"

"No. Honestly I'm telling the truth!" he said. That is the only ghost story I can recall. He never went back to that place again!
Laughter.

Dennis Taylor used to live at the back of us at Beardwood but he remarried and I think he lives in Cheshire now. I photographed him with the trophy in 1985, I think. I also photographed him for a shirt firm, Garstang's, who used to be on Preston New Road. He was their number one customer who wore one of their shirts. I photographed him in one of the firm's rooms where they had a snooker table, a bar and lots of Irish whiskey.

We used to do the glamour pictures for The Daily Sketch and so on. There was a female welder called Anita West. This was in 1964 and she started work at Wilcox Engineering on King Street, training to be a welder. We got her with the welding hat and all the gear on but we made sure that you could see the legs as well to bring the beauty part into it. It went down a bomb with the daily papers. We photographed her a few times. It was a matter of getting that something different.

Did you keep any props in your car?
When we knew we were going to do something we always made sure that we had

the right gear at hand. We did one with John Byrom of the Rovers when he scored a hat-trick. We had him pictured with three bowler hats. You wouldn't be able to do it now. Not unless you had a few thousand quid to give away!

We used to take football players into schools and photograph them with the lads and dress it up a bit. The players were grateful for a copy of the photographs for their scrapbook.

Do you have any more sporting memories?

At Peel Park, Accrington Stanley had to kick off before 2:00pm as they didn't have floodlights. We used to photograph a lot of Stanley's games at Peel Park. Somebody did a book on Stanley. They used my photographs. Some of the pictures showed Peel Park when it was dilapidated and run down. I did the photographs for The Daily Herald and The Sunday People who were owned by the same group.

I remember photographing the Anders twins and their families for cup week. It was offbeat stuff with the players at their daytime jobs. The papers loved offbeat stuff, a postman kicking a ball that type of thing. They were a good set of lads. Mike Ferguson was a good mate of mine. He played for Stanley then signed for Rovers and later played for Aston

Villa and Queens Park Rangers. He was a good player!
When Stanley got their floodlights, blimey there was more light in our bathroom!

I remember Peter Dobing[8] and his wife Judith staying at our house on Winnie Lane the night Judith's dad went missing. They found him in the snow. He had collapsed trying to get home. He lived at Belthorn and he had been to one of the pubs there for a pint. It was a terrible night with very deep snow. My dad rang me up to tell me that a guy had gone missing and it turned out to be Judith's father. My father, Judith and Peter Dobing along with the cops went out looking for the father who had attempted to take a shortcut across a field trying to get home.

Ron Clayton used to room with Duncan Edwards when they both played for England. They were very close. What a fantastic player. I photographed the Manchester United team in November 1957 at Preston for a team group picture. Duncan Edwards was there and all the lads that were in the Munich Disaster.
I remember that match at Preston in those days the players would walk out onto the

---

[8] *Peter Dobing is famous for having played for Blackburn Rovers and Manchester City.*

pitch in their suits or wearing their team blazers about one hour before the kick off to take a look at the pitch.

I remember walking down the tunnel at Preston. Preston then had like an inbetween track where you could walk in between the crowds. The players and the club's directors came out together. Usually then the directors went to their seats

"Can I have your autograph sir?" said this lad to Duncan.

"Don't go bothering him now lad!" said one of the directors.

"Just a minute!" said Duncan. "Certainly son. I'll do that for you right away."

He went over to the lad and this lad's face lit up. I've always remembered that.

I still have that team photograph on a glass plate.

Some of the lads at the Rovers used to have a fag at half time. It was quite normal then. When Fergie (Mike Ferguson) was playing for the Rovers I went as a passenger in his car many times and you would see fag packet after fag packet.

"Don't you ever empty the car?" I'd said to him on many occasions.

"Yes I'll do it Howie," he'd say. "I'll get round to it!"

He never did!

Laughter.

Dougie (Derek Dougan) had put in a transfer request on the eve of Rovers 1960 Cup Final game against Wolves and he played like it too. I took a picture of Dougie at Blackburn Town Hall just sat on his own. There was a row of chairs and nobody sat near him. He just sat there with a cup of tea. The photo went down a bomb when it was published. Why he wanted to leave Rovers I've no idea but his transfer request couldn't have been more ill timed.

There always used to be cliques in the Rovers squad as there are in all work places and the players would play pranks on one another.
I remember when Keith Newton got a call from the England squad. To bring him down to earth one of the Rovers players nailed Keith's boots to a duck board in the dressing room.
Laughter.
Just pranks really. A player would come to put on his tie after the game to find it had been shortened by a pair of scissors.
I used to go to the team meetings. Then we'd go off for a pint. The players would split and discuss in little corners who was going to pull the next prank!
Laughter.

Be it chopping a tie or shirt sleeves, they were buggers!
Laughs.
There used to be a massive bath in the dressing room and there was a toilet nearby. You had to walk past the bath to get to the toilet. If anyone went into the toilet a bucket of water would be filled from the bath water and the water tossed over the cubicle.
Laughter.
Fergie was a bugger and he knew that he'd get his turn after the pranks he pulled. One day he walked past the bath purposely and slowly so that one of the opposite cliques would drown him with a bucket of bath water. The thing they didn't know though was Fergie was wearing one of their own shirts!
Laughter.

I used to go training with the team and the lads would run and jog around the track alongside the main ground. Jack Weddle who was the trainer would blow a whistle and the lads would sprint. He'd blow it again and they'd jog. The lads weren't great trainers and certainly not keen on this jogging and then this sprinting which in their opinion went on too long! So Fergie got his own whistle and he'd blow it and of course the squad would stop their sprinting then either return to jogging or ease up and walk loosening up.

144

Laughter.

Jack would stand there scratching his head and looking at his whistle!

You had to be fit in the days when I photographed the games at Ewood and Burnley or elsewhere for that matter. If I was at one end of the ground and there was a penalty at the other end I would sprint from one end to the other or cut across one corner to another to get the photograph and the crowd would shout *Come on Howard*! Now with 1000 mil lens you just stay in the middle and you have the picture!

I covered the three As boxing for The Daily Express at Belle Vue. My dad photographed Brian London at King George's Hall and he also photographed Randolph Turpin. I still have the pictures.

Do you have memories of any bizarre stories?

I went for a meal recently to the Clog and Billycock and it reminded me of a chap called Walter Salt who was an old chap. He had a pony and trap which he kept just off Billinge. Walter was charged with speeding in it and had to appear in court. Of course this was a good story and we followed it through.

The case was dismissed by the court but the picture potential was excellent. We had

Walter in his pony and trap and we waited at the Clog and Billy for him to come down from where the old cottages are. We told him to give it some leather which he did. The pony and trap passed us then turned round and did it again. This happened three or four times with me and my dad photographing him. We got a great picture of the horse laughing!
We got back to the studio to process the negatives and we made a print.
"Look at that!" my dad said.
"What?" I said.
"All of the horse's hooves are off the floor!"
It wasn't galloping at all it was trotting. Nine times out of ten you would see two feet off the ground. That was so bizarre!
The papers loved that one. That was about 1957.

Did you have to photograph tragic accidents too?
As well as the general newspaper photographs of football games and offbeat pictures of various characters there is the sadder side when there's an accident, fire or drowning incidents. We covered many over the years.
When there has been a family tragedy the newspapers were always hungry for photographs of the deceased and unfortunately we had to get them. We usually

approached a near relative such as a grandparent, brother or sister so we didn't have to go direct to the deceased's home. We would get a nice photograph of the person and pass it around to other papers so a parent or husband or wife wouldn't be bothered by other papers for a photograph.

Tell me about the famous picture of Margo that you took.

There used to be a pet shop at the top of King Street and they had a parrot outside who would give a wolf whistle if a smart young lady walked by.

Margo Grimshaw was a local landlady at the time and very attractive in a mini skirt so what more did we want? We set Margo up to walk by as the parrot in the cage whistled at her. The picture went really well and went in all the daily newspapers that we dealt with at the time.

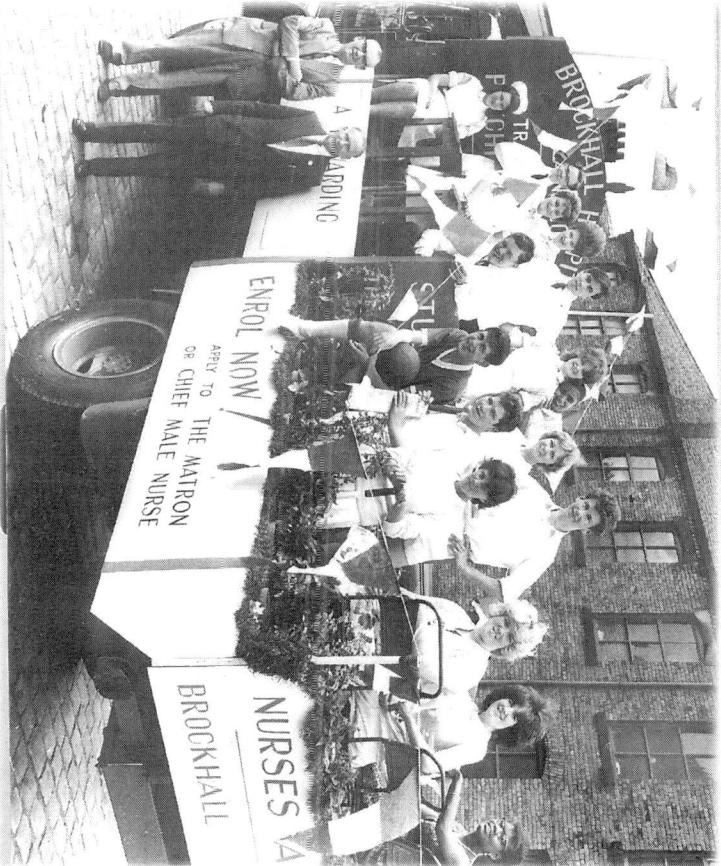

Photographs all printed with the kind permission of Howard Talbot.

Photograph 1: 1956, "Winter Wonderland" in Corporation Park.

Photograph 2: Cyrabel and her driver Walter Salt were followed by a police patrolman on a motorcycle and charged for exceeding the speed limit. When the case came to court it was immediately dismissed for at the time the speed limit did not apply to a horse drawn vehicle. Unusually, not one of Cyrabel's hooves is touching the ground in this picture. Photograph taken in 1957.

Photograph 3: "Blakewater Ball Boy" Ally McLeod of Blackburn Rovers during training for a cup tie on the Little Wembley pitch at Ewood where the ball was often punted into the river. Photograph taken 1958.

Photograph 4: "The photographing Talbots". Son Howard and his father Wally in their studio on Preston New Road. Photograph taken 1983.

Photograph 5: Blackburn Carnival, June 1963. Pictured is the Brockhall Hospital float.

Joan Bell

Born 1928

Were you born in Blackburn Joan?

Yes, in Audley, the Queens Park area. I was born at 27 Pringle Street. It was a two up and two down terraced house. When I was about ten we moved to a house across the road which was a bigger house. That was number 196 Pringle Street.

Do you have any brothers and sisters?

I have an older sister.

Did both of your parents go out to work?

My father served his apprenticeship at Ashton Frost which was a well known engineering company in Blackburn who constructed the Revidge Tank. Unfortunately I never knew where the company was based. There was also Clayton and Goodfellows at the bottom of Audley. That was another engineering firm. My mother used to work at the mill. My mother's family came from Ireland and settled in the Montague Street area of Blackburn.

"Where did my grandma come from?" I once said to my mum.

"What do you want to know that for?" she said.

"I'm just curious!"

"Well mind your own business!"

And that was the end of it.

My dad's family was from Preston and the Fylde. His great grandfather was a gamekeeper.

Did you stay in Pringle Street or did the family move on?

I got married from Pringle Street in 1951 and we just kept to our own community. My mother's parents lived on the next row. Uncle Arthur and his wife lived further up.

Which school did you attend?

I went to Audley Council which was at the back of our house and built in 1928. It was very modern. Intack and Roe Lee schools were built about the same time - I think. I passed my scholarship and then went to Blackburn High School. That was a red brick building that's no longer there. I left school when I was sixteen years old.

What were your favourite subjects at school?

I liked biology, geography and I was good at art but Latin and Algebra - oh dear! However, my sister taught maths when she left school.

What street games would you play?

Hop, spit and stride.

Laughter.

It sounds disgusting!

Laughter.

I suppose we were disgusting doing some of these things.

You'd be slipping all over the place if someone had a cold!

Laughter.

No, because you had a piece of cloth pinned on your chest. There were no tissues then and we couldn't have handkerchiefs, we used to lose them!

Toilet paper was out so we used newspapers cut up into neat little squares. If you had time you threaded them on some string and hung them on the nail of the lavatory door.

My mother's mother used to call it the *W*. I would often go to the *W* at my grandma's and wonder why it was called a *W*. It was only like ours!

Laughter.

Whatever you wish to call them, they were always whitewashed inside and I used to draw on the walls. I'd just disappear for a while and draw!

Not me Joan I'd never hang about, too many spiders for my liking

Laughter.

When we went up market from newspaper we got Izal!
Laughter.
Horrible stiff and smelly!
The joys of those days Joan, Izal toilet paper and Camp Coffee!
I remember Camp Coffee. Tasted like it was made with acorns and vinegar or something!
Laughter.
I think it was chicory but you're not far off!

Can you remember the washing days and baking?
Yes, the dolly tub and posser. Some people had a different name for the posser. Monday was wash day. You would go in the house and there would be washing draped all over the place.
My mum would make barm cakes. We would put butter and treacle on them. That was a treat!
When I was eight or nine another treat was listening to the wireless and BBC's Children's Hour when Romany[9] and his dog Raq were

---

[9] *Romany was the Reverend George Bramwell, 1884-1943. He was a minister of the Methodist Church. His young friends Muriel and Doris, together with Comma the horse and Romany's dog, Raq, accompanied him on his weekly outings.*

on. Romany used to tell you about the countryside and the things that went on in the country. Now whether he was a real gypsy or not I don't know. You had to have a vivid imagination with the wireless, something that is lacking these days.

Did you play any other games as a child Joan?

Yes, tig or some people called it tag; hop scotch; hide and seek; Ralivo and skipping.

Another game was ca led relations. We used to play this from the end house across where there was a Magsons shop as you had to cross the street. There was very little traffic though. One person was *on* and you had to shout out *Aunty Alice* so if you had an Aunty Alice you took a stride, *Uncle Bob*, so you took another. The one who reached the other side of the street first became *on*.

We played lots of different games in the school yard that would be banned now. There was one where a person has their hands flat against the wall and arched their back for everyone to jump on until the whole lot collapses into a heap of bodies!

We used to play buttons which was just tiddlywinks only you would flirt buttons. Marbles was another game we played, depending on the time of the year.

My favourite pastime though was bursting gas tar bubbles in the summer! You could do that in the middle of the street because the only traffic was the old milk cart. If you ever saw a car you would stand and watch it go by.

They used to say that the tar was good for a cold and your chest, so we would stand near the pot that the workmen were boiling up the tar in and breathe it in. Brown paper and goose grease on your chest was a popular remedy when you had a cough that was rather crackly and messy.

Ken Dodd said that his mother used to put mustard plasters on his chest and all the other kids at school would rub their ham sandwiches in it.

Laughter.

I don't know where Ken went to school but all the kids I knew had either cold toast or spam on their butties.

The only entertainment I remember was to go to Park Road Congregational Church for their Christmas Pantomime. Oh that was great. Or grandma would take us to the Savoy Cinema or the Central. If you went up Chester Street you came to the Victoria which was known as Charnley's.

I can remember going to the Majestic when they had a yoyo competition. This would be about 1937 or '38. I think it was a national competition to find the best yoyoist or whatever they're called. About five years ago one of the children at Trinity Church had a yoyo but he couldn't get the thing going, so Elsie who will be eighty six asked to have a go.

He said to her: "Do you know what to do?"

She said: "I think so."

She'd been in this competition. You should have seen his face when she started doing all the tricks!

Laughter.

We used to make our own yoyos. We didn't always have a bought one. We made them using a cotton reel.

Another game was with two sticks with a string across and you had one of these reels. You'd flick it up and catch it again. The boys seemed to play that more.

Did you have a bicycle?

Well I had a red tricycle when I was younger but the only bike I remember having was one that my dad put together.

How about a bogie?

We had what we called a flat wagon which someone pushed from behind with a pole mostly these were owned by the boys.

Where did you get your clothes from?

When I was quite young I had to wear a Welsh Wool hand knitted vest. The wool was untreated. It was smelly and oily. My mother used to knit them. It was like wearing barbed wire. We used to have knitted socks too but we were always warm.

Mr Caruthers on Audley Range was a little hunched backed man who made clogs. He also used to play in one of these little Three Blind Mice orchestras. I think he played the piano.

I wore a liberty bodice with added suspenders when I grew older. We also wore black patent ankle strap shoes, which were bought from Whiteheads shop on Copy Nook.

My mother always made our clothes. The dresses were made with Miss Muffitt print, which was extremely good cotton. If there was a bit of material left over you might have got a pair of knickers to match! I can remember going to Hawkins, which is near where Marks and Spencer is, for the material. It cost 6d. halfpenny a yard. When you paid you gave the lady the money over the counter and it was put into a small cylinder that was then attached to a rail above her head. She then pulled a cord to send it along the rail. It went winging off to the cash office and the change would come back to her the same way!

In the winter when we were small we used to wear gaiters which were like spats with legs. I can remember my mother sitting us on the drainer one at a time and they had about a dozen buttons down the side which she'd do up. My sister said that these came from Field's Ruby Shop on Montague Street.

Another treat was to look through the windows of the City Dairy and watch all the milk coming down these rollers and listen to all those bottles crashing about. The dairy was somewhere round St Anne's Roman Catholic Church.

When we were young my mother told us not to speak to Catholics! I found out about two years ago from a Catholic friend who lived up Queens Park that she was taught not to speak to us!

My grandma, who came from Ireland, was a Catholic, so there was a lot of trouble when she married my granddad who wasn't. My Aunty Nora, my grandma's sister, lived near us and we were told to ignore her if we saw her. She used to wear long black clothes, which a lot of people did then, and always had a black felt hat. We used to think that she was a witch when we were small.

Can you name some brand names that now seem long forgotten?

We used to use Gibbs Pink Dentifrice. It came in a round tin and a solid pink block. It used to froth a lot when you cleaned your teeth. Gibbs referred to your teeth as Ivory towers. My mother used to send coupons off and we would get jigsaw puzzles for them.

Can you remember the shops in Blackburn?

We usually walked down to town. We very rarely caught the tram. Everybody walked in those days. We used to go down to town from the top of Audley where the bridge crosses the canal. My dad used to lift us up to look over the bridge to watch the barges being pulled by the horses. We thought that was great.

On Darwen Street there used to be a confectioner's called Brown's who baked the best brown bread in Blackburn.

There was the Great Universal Stores where the Halifax Building Society is now.

There used to be a toffee shop near our school called Lawson's. On one side of the shop they had toffees. On the other drums of lamp oil, potatoes and firewood. That's the shop that we would spend our Saturday halfpenny in.

Can you remember some of the sweets on offer Joan?

Yes, there were Lucky Horse Shoes which were like a fondant with a small gift inside.

Black Pete was like a caramel liquorish toffee which had a black man's head on the wrapper. I don't think that that would be allowed today.

Spearmint Chews which were like a bright pink ruler. It was ghastly stuff. Really very minty.

My mother would say: "You don't want to buy bubbly gum you know what it's made of don't you? Horse's hooves!" She insisted that bubbly gum was made from horse's hooves.

Laughter.

Dark Virginia, which was shredded coconut, made to look like tobacco and toffee cigarettes. Again you couldn't buy them now.

Kali or if you were posh you would call it sherbet. The kali used to be served from a jar but the sherbet was usually in a yellow packet with a straw for you to suck up the sherbet.

Something that my sister remembers which I don't was that the house next door to the shop had a girl living there who had pneumonia and so you had to be quiet. The front entrance of the house had a closed gate so that you couldn't use it and it wouldn't clang, which would disturb her. On the pavement outside of the house, and in the street, straw was spread to help cushion the sound of people walking by wearing clogs because she was so ill. I don't remember this but my sister remembers it well.

I remember that my mother stopped us playing near Mrs Brown's house on the corner when she was ill. She later died.

Do you remember the tradition of closing the curtains out of respect for a neighbour who had passed away?

Yes of course. I remember coming down the back street from my grandma's and there was a group of people at the end. It was one of these fellows who used to wander round and he had collapsed so someone had called for an ambulance. I didn't go past as I wasn't sure if you were allowed to. I was stood at the top of what we called the slope. The ambulance went up Chester Street after it had picked this man up. Then it disappeared out of view. I was convinced that he had gone to heaven.

When anybody died everybody closed their curtains and somebody always went round the street collecting money for flowers. The men always took their caps or hats off when a funeral passed by.

There was one man who was probably only in his early thirties and his wife died. They had a little boy who I don't think was old enough to go to school. Some women came round collecting.

"What are you going to do with the money?" my mother said.

"We're going to send a wreath," said the woman. "What do you think we'll do?"

"I don't want to give money for a wreath. I'd rather give money to buy that child something to help the father because he's not been able to work."

I think he still got flowers.

Neighbours would take a turn watching and keeping company of people who were very ill. I remember my mother taking her turn to look after an elderly spinster who was on her last legs. About three of the neighbours took it in turn to sit with her during the night.

My grandma died a week or so before the war started, but we had to go to school the same.

Tell me about your job as a textile designer.

I used to create designs that would be turned into the patterns on woven jacquard material; cushion covers, upholstery and all sorts of things.

I worked from 8:30am until 5:30pm for four days a week and until 6:00pm on Thursdays. I went to night school as well so my spending money was increased, but money went a lot further then. I also had to work on a Saturday morning. I got £1 a week.

Mrs Bell (on the right) and her school friends –
known to one another for approximately
eighty years.

Accrington Pipe Band. Mrs Bell is to the right.

Blackburn - In Their Own Words

John Murphy

Born 1935

Let's start with your early recollections John. Where were you born?

Very near the dock area in Liverpool. Where we lived was off Stanley Road. The bottom road was Vauxhall Road. Next to that was the dock area. My name (Murphy) sounds Irish but the family isn't. We're Scottish. My grandmother and grandfather lived in Belthorn.

Do you have any brothers or sisters?

At the present moment I have seven brothers and sisters. There were eight of us. My mum and dad have died. I'm the second eldest and the youngest had their sixtieth birthday a couple of months back.

Three of us were evacuated to Belthorn. The house was bombed that I was in. We left there and went to my Grandmother's.

Can you go back a bit to your days in Liverpool? What did your dad do for a living?

Originally he was a seafarer - sailing to America and Canada.

What was his job on board the ship?

He did all sorts, whatever he was needed to do. His father was the same. He went to sea with his father. My mother used to work as a sewing machinist.

Did you go to school in Liverpool?

No, I was only three or four years of age then. I was baptised at St Alphonce's Church which was just a little down from where we lived.

Was your house a terraced house?

They were all terraced. It was actually two up three down, kitchen, living room and what we called the parlour then. It was a typical working class area and an Irish area too but, as I said, my grandparents were both Scots.

What year was that first bomb that destroyed your home dropped?

1939, just after the start of the war.

You were very young at the time. Do you remember the incident?

I was just under five year old. Oh yeah, I can remember it very, very well. My sister Teresa was two years older than me and is seventy five now. Margaret was two years younger than me. It was late on in the evening and they were bombing all round. It was an incendiary bomb that hit the house.

Did you have an air raid shelter?

We had one in the street at the front of the house. Each street had an air raid shelter.

So your family was fortunate enough to get out in time when the sirens were heard?

Sometimes the shelters were completely full. My dad was on nights. At the time he worked on the docks - after the sea faring. Then all men of that age had to go on night watch.

Were you in the shelter at the time of the bombing?

No, under the table. Most people in those days went under the table with a mattress on top to take the shock and protect against flying shrapnel. Then they would surround it with things the best way that they could. After the third attempt my mum and dad had enough of it. They brought us up to Belthorn. Quite a lot of the family from Liverpool were living at Belthorn.

Where did the bomb hit?

The back end of the house, the kitchen and very close to the living room.

Were you dug in?

Yes.

Your family must have been terrified?

It was frightening, but as children we didn't understand quite what was happening.

What happened after you knew that your home had been hit?

We just stayed there until it quietened off a bit. The Ak Aks were going up and the search lights.

Was the living room destroyed so bad that you couldn't get out?

Well we had to stay there because of the shelling outside. You can't just walk out into the street with bombs still dropping. We just had to wait until we got the all clear. I can remember the house across the road being hit and people being buried underneath. A lot of people used their cellars in an air raid as an air raid shelter if you will. These people that were in the cellar died under there.

Can you describe the shelters in the street?

They were big shelters, wide and long, no electric at all. They were cold and damp. I should think the only heat came off the people huddled in there. From what I can recall there were boards for kids to sleep on, or for the elderly to sleep. I don't think that torches were allowed but I think some people may have brought stools or chairs in.

Where did you go to live after the bombing?

When we got out at about eleven to midnight we went to live at my grandmother's house.

Was your house now completely unfit and unsafe to occupy?

It wasn't a complete right off. The back was burnt down and obviously once that's gone there would be no cooking facilities and I think that one of the bedrooms had gone. I don't think it was inhabitable.

Did the bomb actually go off or was the shear weight of the thing enough to cause the damage?

It was a firebomb and incendiary. But there were other bombs dropped around there that night in Stanley Road and Scotland Road. We went to grandma's in Thompson Street. Quite a lot of my grandmother's family met there as their own houses had been bombed too, so we all lived there. That house was bombed and I was there, but that was a proper bomb. This was in a couple of days of being bombed out of our own home.

How many were in the house on this occasion?

I think there were about fifteen or twenty of us. This was a night time raid too.

Where were you this time?

We were in the basement that time. A cellar is a different thing from a basement. In a cellar you go down the stairs and it's enclosed. The basement you could get out of the back door.

So your grandma's house was a lot bigger than your own?

Quite a lot bigger. I think it was three stories high. Nobody got hurt I recall. My grandmother had quite a lot of food and that was wasted, full of soot and what have you. There were one or two of her sons in the forces at that time or maybe a son-in-law. They were on leave. They of course helped out as they were young men.

It's a wonder that you don't have nightmares about this John!

It doesn't bother me now. We may have had nightmares when we went to Belthorn.

Where did you move to after this incident?

To another house! It was a case of going into shelters, coming out of shelters, find somewhere else to live. I can't go any further than the third house because that's when we were shipped off to Belthorn.

What age were you when you arrived in Belthorn?

I arrived in Belthorn on my fifth birthday, the 16th February, with the two sisters. I was at one house and my sisters were at another, next door to one another.

***How did your family come to live in
Belthorn, which must have been fairly
isolated in those days, after living in a large
city as Liverpool?***

I can't understand how they found Belthorn in
the first place - having come from a place like
Liverpool. My wife has been trying to find a
book on Belthorn. I can remember it being
twenty foot deep in snowdrifts. We had a
photograph, it's in a book, of a double decker
bus under the snow. So you can imagine how
bad it was.

Did you move to your grandparent's house?

No. It was a cousin's house. They were called
Hornby.

Have you still got family living in Belthorn?

I only know of maybe one of the Hornbys.
Their children will still be alive. But I only
know one of the Hornbys. I think he moved to
Bolton. Other than that we lost track of them.

Where about in Belthorn did you live?

Do you know Belthorn? We lived down the
bottom of a road called The Rann in
Hutchinson Street. They're terraced cottages.
They're still there. My sisters lived with a lady
called Marjorie. Times were very hard. The
winters were vicious. It was an entirely
different environment to Liverpool.

Across the road from us was a Labour Club. It's not a Labour Club now. Down at the bottom of the street was a farm. I can't recall the name of the farm but every day cows were brought out and taken up the hill for grazing in the fields. Of course the road was completely filled with cow pats! It was an excepted thing, cows on the footpath and the main road.

Did your parents stay in Liverpool?

Yes, they stayed in Liverpool another six months apparently. Then after six months we left Belthorn.

Did you go to school in Belthorn?

Yes, I went to St Michael's. In those days the school had maybe two teachers and you went from being five to when you were eleven. Then you moved on to other schools. In fact, one is in the Accrington area in Oswaldtwistle, Rhyddings.

You went to Rhyddings School?

No, other kids did. We were a Catholic family and ninety nine percent of the village were either Methodists or Church of England. There were two churches. One on the top and one half way down, but no Catholic church. We were "red necks".

So where did you worship as Catholics?
We didn't until we moved down to Guide. One of the Churches in Blackburn bought a house near Queens Park Hospital which was turned into a kind of chapel.

Can you remember the names of any of your class mates from St Michael's?

I can only give you that from the Belthorn book. I do believe that I'm on one of the photographs. One of the families was Gabbuts. They married one of my cousins. They were a well known family. I think they must have originated in the village. They go back years and years. There are still some of the old Belthorn people still there.
There was a family called Chambers.
Go down the lanes and there is a big mansion and there was a family called Winders living there. They were solicitors. I believe the house is still there but I haven't been round there for years. I didn't enjoy my time in Belthorn, but after a number of years we used to go up there visiting with dad. I used to go for a pint with him and I really loved them times and I still love the place now. But at the time, those six months there, I hated it. They were all foreigners to us coming as we did from Liverpool - their speech for instance!

177

"Thee can't speak King's English thee!" they'd say in a broad Lancashire dialect!
"Tha's a foreigner. Tha comes from Ireland. Tha's gypsies thee!"
We were complete outsiders.

Tell me about your move to Guide John.
Guide was another non-Catholic area. There was one Catholic family already there when we moved to Guide but they kept quiet about it!
Laughs.
There was a school there, St James', which is no longer there. All the schools I've been to are now all gone.
I lived at 159 School Lane. The first house we lived in. It was a two up, two down with no back door! You know where the motorway is now? Well there were four cottages. I think there's only two there now. What we called the sink, wash basin or "slop stone" was a hole and it ran into the grate outside. We had cold water and one gas light in the front room. None in the rest of the house and a gas stove in the back kitchen. We had an old range, an oven on one side with a boiler on the other. The grate had an arm on it where we would boil the kettle.
We had never seen anything so old. This was jungle living, if you will. My two sisters lived with us now - and a brother, Tom.

Do you know who owned the cottage originally?

No, but I know that my dad was offered the four cottages, if he wanted to buy them for a hundred pounds. There were now four of us and my mum and dad.

How did you come to move to Guide?

There was a chance somehow to move to our own house as dad and mum had heard that there was a cottage empty there. It was the only one at the time so they took the chance for the family to be together.

It must have been a big move for your dad to move jobs from working on the docks?

He got a job in Blackburn at Northrop where they made the looms. He was working there labouring.

I imagine that the pay would have been poor compared to working on the Liverpool docks?

It was terrible! You were rained off when it was raining and you didn't get paid. I know they were very hard times. Either end of the cottages there were two tubs which were round with a board across. Now two families shared those tubs. Two families on one side and two families on the other side. You can imagine there were six of us in the family and next door there were two people next door to us - and these toilets were empted every fortnight! When the snow came, and I'm talking snow, they couldn't be empted as they couldn't get up to us. So if you wanted to go to the toilet you would cross the road and climb up the snow and go wherever you could!

Can you remember any of your class mates' names from St James' Guide?

I can remember a lot of them. The Miltons, Gregorys, Aldritt and Heap. Eric Milton, I think, took a pub in Darwen and he's still around. The Gregorys were a well established family in the village. Their father was an overlooker. What they used to call a tackler in the mill.

Did your cottage originally belong to a mill owner?

The first one we lived in was a miner's cottage. Apparently they were earmarked for demolition during the 1914-18 war. They should have been pulled down then. The second house we went to, further down into Guide, that had electric lighting that was fantastic. It also had flush toilets! That was a mill house, number 38 School Lane. We lived more or less directly across from the school.

Can you remember how many classes they had at the school?
Only two classes.

The headteacher, without saying too much about him, he was a right B! He was called Thompson. He was very old, from the 1890s or 1900s. He was very Victorian, a vicious man. He carried a cane and would lay into you.

Mrs Johnson, on the other hand, was an exceptionally nice woman. She was a teacher. These were the only teachers in the school. They taught from when you were four years of age until you were eleven. After that you went to Blakey Moor or St Peter's.

What sort of entertainment was available for the villagers?
There was the Con Club, which is still there. One of the families I gave you the Gregorys, well Maurice Gregory, who died a couple of years ago, ran the Con club. It was very active in those days as most of Guide was Conservative. Then there was the King Edward. The landlord there was called Ross Walker. This would be in about 1941. He was there for a number of years.

What did you do for entertainment as a lad?

There was a big green area at the back of the pub or at the back of the cottages where they had roundabouts and things. The men of the village mainly had their garden or plots, hens or what have you.

I can remember some more of the names of the villagers who were neighbours, Juddy, his name was Jesse, Jesse Duerdan. They used to call him Juddy. Another one was Levi Hal. These are names that you don't hear now. There was Rubin Whitwell. All biblical Christian names. Happy, there was an old chap called Happy.

I imagine that a large percentage of the village was related to each other?

I'll give you a point on that! They used to say that if you kicked someone in Belthorn, then half of Guide would limp! So if you fell out with your neighbour you fell out with the rest of the village!

How did your mother and father take to living in a small village like Guide after coming from Liverpool?

They weren't over keen on it. They moved here for the sake of their children. After the war we got word back that Liverpool Council that there was a house available for us.

My dad said to my mum: "What do you think? They're settled here now the kids. Do you want to go back?"

My mother said: "Well no."

And that was it. The family stayed here. It was the greatest move my mum and dad ever made for us. Mum and dad settled here rather than Liverpool.

You mentioned that your cottage was a mill cottage, but where was the mill?

Right at the cross from the King Edward Spring Bank? I can't remember. There was also one right across from us in Belthorn where we lived. That's still there now.

What was there before Whitbread built their site in Guide?

It was known as Pit Fields. There's a mine underneath that. It was actually part of a farm called Capsticks. On that land there were a lot of Italian prisoners of war.

Was this an enclosed prisoner of war camp?

No, from all accounts they slept in the barn. They never made any attempt to run away. They were better off here than fighting. They were probably guarded by the Home Guard who had rifles but no bolts in them! It was a case of them wondering around the village and going for a pint or going into town. I can remember they used to have these brown suits with big yellow patches on the backs and legs so they could be easily identified. A few of them went back home after the war and came back and settled here.

There was a woman called Mrs Rimmer in the village. Her husband had cleared off and left her and two weeks later her brother died in Queens Park Hospital. She had no family other than that. She had a son called Sam who was nineteen, a really good looking lad who was sent out to El Alamain.

He said to my mum: "I won't be coming back."

She said: "Don't be silly!"

On the Monday Mrs Rimmer, Maggie Rimmer, passed my mum the telegram! Within a month she had lost her husband, brother and son.

What school did you go to after the Guide village primary school?

We went down to St Mary's Catholic School, which is where the post office sorting office is now on Canterbury Street. The school's down now so is the church where my wife and I got married in 1966. At aged eleven I left St Mary's and went to St Alban's higher grade.

Do you have fond memories of your time at St Mary's?

The headmaster was a bit harsh. We used to call him Tommy Tucker. His name was

Turner. He could be a bit vicious at times. I remember him laying into a lad with a stick and leaving him so he couldn't walk.

What subjects were you good at?

Very few actually.

Laughs .

Geography was probably my best subject, with my dad travelling the world and giving me all the information as to where he'd been. He'd been to New York and mixed with Mafia.

Laughs.

He actually did mix with gangsters, Legs Diamond, and one or two others. He jumped ship. He left Liverpool crossed the Atlantic and got fed up and jumped ship in New York. He got mixed up with various people during the prohibition. Of course gangsters were behind the illegal supply of booze in them days. I think he met about three top ones, Machine Gun Kelly and Legs Diamond. That Scar Face, he met him, but didn't get involved with him.

Did he make a lot of money out of this?

I don't think he did, no. If he did he spent it all. His mother paid a lot of money in those times, the 1920s, to have him shanghaied, if you will, back to Liverpool. She paid two of his friends about fifty pounds to get him back again. My grandparents were very wealthy people. She paid his friends to get him "popped up" and back on board a ship. When he arrived home he said he'd never sail again!

What was your source of entertainment as a teenager and what music did you listen to?

I liked singers such as Al Jolson and Bing Crosby. This would be about 1944.

When my dad was at sea, and he went to the United States, each trip back he would bring records. They'd usually be ones that you just couldn't get over here like opera singers and what have you.

On sunny days, when he was younger, he would bring the old gramophone out into the street and the lads and girls of his own age would have a dance in the street to the popular music of the day.

Were you a cinema goer?

I think I went to every cinema in town at some point. The one at the bottom here used to be called The Barn (now Thwaites theatre). I'd been to The Rialto, The Royal, The Majestic, The Palace, The Star (Little Harwood), The Palladium (Mill Hill), The Central and The Olympia across from one another.

Where did you work when you left school?

I left when I was fifteen and went straight into the cotton mill at Fernhurst Mill. I worked in cotton mills most of my working life, forty five or more years. I started off as a reacher, then a loomer, then a twister or knotter as they're known.

You don't seem to have been affected by the occupational deafness suffered by many mill workers?

I am actually. I'm severely deaf and have two hearing aids which I very seldom use. It can be very painful at times. I worked mainly at Fernhurst Mill. As a mill shut down you'd move on to another mill. If you couldn't get work in a mill you'd try anywhere.

Did you do any National Service John?

I signed up for three years actually but I failed the medical unfortunately. I had a bad hernia and that was through the mill work.

I imagine around this time that many of your pals were called up?

They were but with having this bad hernia from lifting a beam I missed out. I would have liked to have gone in.

Did you go to any of the town centre dance halls?

I went to Tony's and King George's Hall. I used to go around with a chap who played the sax at Tony's.

Going back to your childhood in Guide, tell me about the chap who kept hens.

Oh you mean Cock Sunter. They called him that because he had a small holding at the back of his house with hens and cocks. Cock Sunter actually lived in Belthorn. The Sunters were all related to one another, both in Guide and Belthorn, farmers and small holders. I think there were butchers too in the family.

Did your dad have a plot?

Yes, he kept hens, ducks and geese and he grew vegetables too. That was in Guide.

So you were fairly self sufficient during the war years and the post war period?

Fairly. Come Christmas time I was expected to neck something for the Christmas table. Not to mention cleaning it out.

Did your mum and dad go in the Conservative Club or The King Edward?

My dad used both Belthorn and Guide. Belthorn for the reason during the war that when my parents visited us they wouldn't let us see them to prevent us from getting upset.

They went into the Dog Inn in Belthorn. Mrs Martin and her husband had the pub then. Then you could stop at the top of Belthorn and look down towards Liverpool and see it all ablaze. Likewise Manchester.

On a number of occasions Mrs Martin told us to sleep at the pub. When heavy raids were on, they put my mum and dad up on the benches around the lounge.

My dad always said: "For what you've done for us we'll repay you one way or another."

So when the family came up they always went there.

The King Edward on the other hand, well, all pubs in those days had pianos. It was great music. People would get up singing. Ross Walker had that. He was a grand chap.

All the entertainment for the lads in the village, for lads of around nine to fourteen, on dark nights, was to go into the side door of the pub, a crowd of you, and scream and shout. Of course this used to wind Ross up. My dad was very friendly with Ross.

Other entertainment for the same group of lads would be Nick Knock. I was one of the smaller kids at the time. We wore clogs with steal toe caps and we would really kick a front door. We'd then leg it whilst the bigger lads would continue kicking as they ran off. By the time the younger kids had run past a door the owner would be out on the step ready to clout you one! If you were a little bit wiser as soon as the words Nick Knock came up you'd start running!

Were there a lot of children living in Guide at this time?

Oh yes, about twenty or thirty. The farmers' sons at that time were allowed to be off school to get the hay in. Also at that time Irish labourers were employed to get the hay in too. They were paying reasonably good rates of pay too. They lived in the barns and would get their meals too. At the end of the summer they would send their money back home or wait maybe six weeks then take it home.

The Irish workers were mainly from Southern Ireland. They could earn maybe two or three weeks wages in one week on the farms over here. There were a lot in and around Guide. They would spend money in the pubs too of course, but a lot of them were tea total having taken the pledge. They wore badges from some temperance movement. Some would go into town for a drink or two. I can't say I recall hearing of any trouble. They mainly kept themselves to themselves.

There was a lane nearby known as the *Divellin* or *The Devil's Lane*. There's a house on the corner, a lane, then you come up towards Guide and it was supposed to have been struck by the devil of something. Carry on down there and there was a place called Slack Gate. A chap used to grow tomatoes and vegetables.

Crime was unheard of then. Most of the houses and cottages in Guide were left unlocked.

Can you remember any other evacuees in either of the villages of Belthorn and Guide?

I can't remember anyone else apart from us. I seem to remember somebody came from down south but they didn't stay very long.

Just going back to St Alban's higher grade, the first week I started, there was a lad from Liverpool. Of course when you hear the accent it was a case of what part of Liverpool do you come from?

The following day my mother asked me the same question as his mother asked him: "What his mother's name?"

His mother was called Katie Slade. My mother's maiden name was Dodd. Believe it or not she was supposed to have been some relation to Ken Dodd!

Of course we both met again the following day.

"What is your mother's name?" he said.

"Molly Dodd"

My mother thought it was that!"

"What was your mother's name?"

"Katie Slade."

They went to the same school in Liverpool! They were two of the best friends! Their third best friend was Cilla Black's mother (born Priscilla White). They knocked about together at St Sylvester's. That's where quite a few of the Liverpool comedians went too.

One particular winter in Guide we were all listening to the wireless around a big fire - with the lights out. It was freezing outside. I was causing a bit of a disruption.

"Any more of that and you're outside!" my dad said.

I carried on anyway!

"Get out!" he shouted.

So out I went in the freezing cold. I thought I'd get my own back on him. So I went round the back of the cottage. The cottage was only so high. I could climb on it and I went onto the kitchen roof then onto the main roof - taking a bucket of water with me.

Can you imagine a big fire burning in the grate and the family sat around it? Well I poured the bucket full of water down the chimney! My dad came out looking like Al Jolson, a jet black face and white teeth. He looked up and called me a fatherless child or something like that!

John with his grandchild.

John on his twenty first birthday.

Elizabeth Stancliffe

Born 1912

Tell me about your childhood days.
I came over from Canada when I was ten
months old.

Were your parents Canadian citizens?
They were Blackburnians who lived in
Edenfield before emigrating to Canada. They
went to Canada in 1910. In those days you
were given a piece of land a mile square and
if you worked it for five years it became your
own. The land was in Prospect Valley,
Alberta. The nearest town was Wainwright. I
was born in 1912. My mother died when I
was three weeks old.
At this time there were many Canadian
Indians roaming around. My mother
welcomed and befriended them. She would
give them material for making clothes. This is
what my father told me. When my mother
died the Indians wanted to adopt me so I
could have well been a squaw!
Laughs.
On the next piece of land was a very wealthy
American family called Jaunderbilt and they
wanted to adopt me too. Instead my father

decided to send a note to his parents and
when I was ten months old my maternal
grandmother brought me to Blackburn. I have
lived here since June 1913.

Were you an only child?

Yes, but my father remarried. He came over
during the First World War. He did want to
join the Canadian army but his heart wasn't
good so they wouldn't take him. He married
his cousin but they didn't have any children.
She died too so he married once more during
the Second World War.

Where in Blackburn did you come to live from Canada?

Well my grandparents lived in Cedar Street at
number 26 and I went to Cedar Street School
when I was four and a half. It was a
marvelous school - very much in advance of
the other schools at that time. Cedar Street
had two schools, the infant school at the top
of the yard and the seniors at the bottom. The
headmistress at the top was called Kate
Whalley. At the bottom school it was Mr
Simpson.

James Simpson was a very outgoing person.
By the time I got to standard five I was doing
Latin. We had an outing once a year to the
Lake District by charabanc. I can remember it

very well. When I was eleven years old we were all waiting at the bottom of St James' Road for this vehicle to appear and somebody told me that the post had come to our house and that I had passed my scholarship to the high school. The year that I went to the high school, five girls passed their Eleven Plus and two boys. We had this grounding in Latin and also we had done a lot of Shakespeare. We went to see a company called Ben Greet, who were a travelling Shakespeare company, when they were at King George's Hall. Different schools went along to see them. The Henry Baynton players were a similar company at this time.

We had a lot of music too. At Cedar Street the deputy head Mr Duxbury and Mr Simpson were very musical. I am the most unmusical person going! What I did benefit from was their love of music and I still like Gilbert and Sullivan which we did a lot of. Before it moved to the Hawthorns or whatever it's called from Cedar Street, there was a little paragraph in the paper about the centenary of Cedar Street School. The little ones were producing a booklet. The article asked for old scholars who had memories of their time at the school. I did an article for the book and they kindly sent me a copy.

When we were in the top class it was divided into two forms, Standard Seven and Standard

Seven X. The Eleven Plus was very new at this time. Before that selected pupils at the junior schools were sent to either QEGS or the High School. At my time it couldn't have been going very long because we had this preliminary exam in the school with maths and English and if you got enough marks in those you went to the Education Office for an oral exam. There was a panel of about five people and I remember Miss Gardner who was the headmistress at the high school when I went there and was on this panel. I even remember after reading something she said to me: "What does the passage mean, it went in a sensible descent?" I must have explained it all right as I was accepted.
Laughs.
Isn't it funny how you remember things from all those years ago?

My grandmother died when I was thirteen and I kept house for my bachelor uncle and my grandfather. When I was eighteen granddad became very morbid so we went to live with my father and his second wife. My father wanted to go back to Canada but my father's second wife wouldn't go back to Canada with him as she didn't want to leave her mother, although the land over there was still his.

What did your father do for a living in Canada?

Farming of course, on the ranch, but the first winter that they were there he worked for Canadian Pacific Railway. They built their own homestead and I have a photograph of it and me near a horse. They also had a cow for milk and butter which was sold in Wainwright.

Were the Indians that you mentioned earlier from a reservation nearby?

No there was no reservation at that time. The Indians just called by periodically.

Father went back to working in a mill when he returned to England. He was a tackler at Stanley Street Mill. Just before the war he bought a cottage in Barker Lane, Mellor and acquired a poultry farm. He got a letter when he was still married to Rose, his second wife, asking him did he still want to keep the land in Canada because they hadn't heard from him for years, but he wrote back and said no. It was actually my mother's brother who had emigrated some time later on. He pulled a fast one because the land was oil rich, which he obviously knew. My father would have been a millionaire!

The poultry business was just over the road. In fact they built Seven Acre Garage on the site of the poultry farm. My father kept the poultry until the middle of the war. We built an air

199

raid shelter on the site. The Evening Telegraph came up to take a picture of it, it was that good. This would be about 1941 or '42.

Can you remember any shops on Cedar Street?

On the corner of Walnut Street and Cedar Street was a grocer called Turner's which everyone went to. I remember my granddad when he wasn't well always had threepenny worth of Indian Brandy. I remember in the winter my grandmother always used to think that we ought to take brimstone and treacle. It was quite usual in those days to go to the grocers for patent medicine.

Where did you live when you got married?

When we first got married, we lived in Whinney Lane, right at the very top in a cottage. Miss Williams lived with her mother and brother in a detached house just below. She was an uncertified teacher at Cedar Street School. My grandfather was a caretaker at Cedar Street. When he retired my uncle Harry took over. He was a wonderful man. When I was pregnant with Peter my first son, she said: "I don't know how Elizabeth will cope, she never could knit!"
Laughs.
And I still can't knit!

What games did you play as a child?

All the games that were played in or out of school had to have seasons. One time we would be playing with skipping ropes then that would finish and it would be marbles. How or who determined this I don't know. It just happened!

I remember particularly, we used to play a game called Trust and how on earth we managed not to break our backs I don't know! One person would lean against the wall in a piggyback position and you would line up and jump on the back over that person and this would keep going until the pile of bodies collapse into a heap. Then you would start again and you would hear someone say *Trust Coming*. Would this be allowed today in the playground?

Another game was Scraps. You had a book and you bought these scraps which were pictures that you would cut out and stick in a page of the book. Then someone would have a pin and they would prick the book. If they got a page with a picture they could keep it, but you kept the pin. What on earth you did with all these pins I've no idea!

One time I was given sixpence (two and a half pence) all at once to spend on scraps. We all got our Saturday pennies and I suppose I was spoilt as I was this child from Canada, this

British Canadian who had no mother. My grandmother gave me two pence a week to spend (one pence) and my father gave me sixpence. I was supposed to give two pence for the Children's Newspaper. My uncle would go for his papers and naturally pay for mine at the same time but eventually my father found out about this two pence and I was made to feel a thief. However, I was the proud processor of eight pence a week which was a fortune.

I also loved to read The Children's Newspaper. It was very good. It had the world news in it[10].

Tell me about your husband.

My husband had a shop which was on the corner of Shear Brow. It was James Stanclffe's. Before that it was Dawson's. The business was a well known high class shoe shop. My husband served his time making footwear as well as repairing them at Marston Boot & Shoe Maker. My son worked at Barratt's shoe

---

[10] *The Children's Newspaper, subtitled "The Story of the World Today for the Men and Women of Tomorrow", ran for an incredible forty six years from its first publication in 1919. It was edited by Arthur Mee and was printed every week.*

shop on King William Street until he went to David Reid Ltd., then he went on his own.

Where did you work?
I went working for a firm of accountants called Thomas Leech at Richmond Chambers and then his son who was also named Tom joined the firm. There was an older son called Jack who came working with us but he had to go into the navy during the Second World War. He was drowned in the Mediterranean.
Tom carried on as a chartered accountant and then joined a company that was to specialise in providing capital for Higher Purchase called Coulthard, Grimshaw and Leech. They could be still in business, but I'm not sure.

What are your memories of World War Two?
I remember more about the rationing and how you made the butter go further by mixing corn flour and milk. We did very well actually as we had a very good grocer at the end of Holland Street on Shear Brow. By then we had moved to Langham Road and I was married.
I had an evacuee in 1943, a mother and her daughter who came from London. The daughter, Gloria, was the same age as my son Norman. Fioranda was the name of the mother which was Italian, Fioranda Goode.

Gloria was a screamer so my three boys went off girls completely!

Fioranda's husband was in a sanatorium in Maidstone in Kent with TB, which he had picked up whilst he was in the ARP. He had to dig out bodies from the London Blitz so mother and daughter came to Blackburn along with other evacuees. During her stay with Jim and me, Fioranda supplemented her income by doing silk work which was on a frame, making these mats out of silk. They were very lovely.

How did Fioranda manage to get hold of the silk?

That's what I'm coming to! It was on points so you could get the material if you had the coupons.

When she came she said: "I shall get another set of ration books for Gloria and me, sweet coupons and clothing coupons."

I said: "You have got them!"

She replied that she would say that they had got *lost* in the Blitz!

At this time you had to have someone in authority to sign that they had been lost. Most of our friends at the time were in this position to sign.

"Fioanda, you won't be asking any of our friends!" I said.

"Oh no, I shall go to the priest at Sacred Heart," she said.

So off she went to Sacred Heart and he signed so that's how she managed to get the silk. She had two ration books!

Did you keep in touch with Fioranda and her family?

Yes, for quite a long time. She had another baby then the correspondence just fizzled out. I remember going to the shop for our rations.

"Oh Mrs Stancliffe would your like some lamb's liver?" the butcher said. I didn't really want it because we managed to get loads of meat.

"Yes it will do for the cat."

"Well I like that! All the other customers are really grateful and you say you'll give it to the blooming cat!"

Laughs.

I remember we got so much meat we didn't know what to do with it. We went on holiday to Morecambe and stayed in a boarding house. When they carved the Sunday joint, all the other customers had a slice of beef, and thought how lovely.

Jim and I looked at it and we commented: "What a small portion!"

Holiday makers would take their own food for the land lady of the guest house to cook. Yes, I remember going away with my stepmother and father and we took tinned pears. When we got to Morecambe, where we mostly went, we would go to the butcher's for a joint and the landlady cooked it.

For the armistices after World War One, I was with my grandparents in Blackpool. Grandfather had been ill so we went for a week for him to convalesce. I can remember when peace was signed. All these people were on the promenade and one of the pubs brought out a piano onto the pavement and everyone was singing and dancing. I was six then and I can remember it very vividly.

We went quite a lot to either Blackpool or Morecambe.

What else can you remember about the period of The Great War?

I can remember my father's youngest brother, Bill. He had three brothers. I can remember standing with my grandma opening the top draw of the sideboard which was narrow long drawer. I can see her now she took out some papers and said: "Don't forget these Will and come back safe and sound."

She was very emotional. He did come back although he was wounded quite a bit. I can remember my Uncle Jack, who was the eldest brother, coming home on leave. He lived next door to my grandparents. When he was on leave we would all get together and he would tell us all these stories about what had happened in France and the hospitals. They were always very light-hearted stories and not the bad things - the funny side of things. This was surprising as he was the sort of man who grumbled a lot!

Laughs.

Tell me what you remember about Blackburn during this period.

I can remember the Easter Fair very well and the pots in particular. The sellers would have all these plates on their arm and they never broke any! Then they had a Dutch auction starting at a couple of pounds, and then went down to shillings. I can remember my Grandfather talking about the Easter Fair. Although it was still illegal, he remembered when he was very young, someone bringing a bear for bears dancing. He said that it was on Victoria Street. They had a lot of sideshows on there in my day. They advertised all sorts of things like chickens with two heads, but I never saw them.

I used to go to the Star Cinema too with my cousin who was seven years older than me. I must have been very naive because she had a boyfriend and she only took me as a cover up!

We know that the town has changed since these far off years but do you think that people have changed too?

I can't really speak for the younger people because all my contemporaries are quite old and think the same way that I do. I can remember very well my stepmother's mother who was called Jane saying she didn't know what young people were coming to these days. We are still saying the same thing today so nothing has changed has it?

Did your family have the traditional family get togethers around the piano?

Well we didn't have a piano but when my parents went to Canada my mother took her organ with her! I never asked my father how they managed to move it from one place to another. I think of these wagon trains and I wonder how they managed with it across the prairie, which takes three days even now by train from Toronto to Calgary!

My father did his best to bring music into my life. He took me to the opera a lot. I still enjoy music but I don't appreciate it as a really musical person would. I suppose I like the story.

Can you remember some of the neighbours in the street during your childhood days?

I can't remember much really. I know that the street was in a lower middle class to working class area and very respectable. Our next door neighbour was called Alf Loynds. He was a police sergeant. Down the road were the McCartneys. Mr McCartney was a police inspector.

During the depression the people around us didn't appear to be bothered unduly and as a girl I had a number of holidays. Uncle Harry was a weaver at Wharf Street Mill. Both he and my father went to the Technical College.

My father became a tackler when he was twenty one, which was very young apparently. In 1936 he got involved in the poultry business on Barker Lane where he lived from 1936 until 1956.

Can you tell me more about your family?

Ray, one of my relatives, did some research on part of the family and discovered that one of our forebears was the vicar of Whalley. He was noted because he could balance a tankard of beer on his head without spilling it. The other bit of notoriety was that he buried people according to Roman Catholic rites yet he wasn't a Catholic himself. He was just a sympathiser. He died in office so evidently wasn't found out. His name is on the board of vicars in Whalley Church.

My mother lived in Walnut and went to school at Troy Street. It became the Whalley Range School of Domestic Science.

How did you spend Christmases?

Christmas was great. It was always a big family occasion. If you couldn't all fit around the table you had two sittings. Everybody came and we always had a goose. The goose grease was always saved for whenever you got a cold. If you caught a cold in winter they always rubbed your chest with goose grease. It went on a piece of brown paper and it was pinned to your vest it smelt horrible!

All the family came to Christmas dinner. There must have been twenty or thirty people. We would play games and sing. Grandma would always sing Farmer's Boy. It was her favourite song. Grandfather would always sing Grandfather's Clock. I think I sang - to everybody's horror! I couldn't sing but I was very good at recitation and recited About Ben Adam.

This is digressing. Every Sunday I had to get a tea with my father and stepmother. Her uncle lived next door. If I went in there and recited About Ben Adam he gave me threepence so I would recite that until the cows came home!

This is what we did at Christmas and my Uncle Bill, my father's younger brother, used to take me round to all my relations. Every house that I called at Father Christmas had left me a present!

Laughs.

One Christmas my father said I was doing too much reading and it was spoiling my eyes, so that Christmas I didn't get a single book. I was relying on receiving all these annuals – Chatterbox, School Girls and others. That was the worst Christmas I can remember. I was eight then.

You hung a pillowcase up, not a stocking. We had a big fireplace and it was hung on there somewhere. I always wanted a stocking because I had never had one so I was bought one by a family friend. It was one of those net ones. I was eleven at the time.

Elizabeth sat on her Aunt Annie's knee as a child.

The homestead at Ribstone, Alberta.

Grandma Catlow, Jennie, Elizabeth and Lady!

Elizabeth around 1955.

Jim Whittle

Born 1940

Where were you born Jim?

I was born in Charnley Street. That's at Waterfall - 21 Charnley Street. That house was especially built for the family. It had haylofts, a washhouse, six stables and a stable yard and it was built for the family. No other family ever lived in that house. They've knocked it down now.

All the rest of the street were just two up, two down. Our place was in the middle of the street. My granddad lived there until his death in 1936 and my dad got married in 1939 and he moved into there. My grandma and my aunty, who never got married, moved into a two up, two down property.

When my dad retired he bought a little bungalow and me and our Dorothy moved back into Charnley Street. It was a proper family house with three bedrooms and a bathroom. My dad wouldn't have an inside toilet. He said it smells!

Laughter.

So we had to go under the hayloft to the toilet.

Did you have any brothers or sisters Jim?
I had one brother and he worked in the coal
job too.

Which school did you attend?
I went to St Aiden's School on Norfolk Street
in Mill Hill. That was a primary school. Then I
left there and went to Blakey Moor Secondary
Modern School. I finished there when I was
about fifteen. I couldn't get away fast enough!
Laughter.
I was more interested in going to work than I
was in going to school.

Did you get a call up for National Service?
I missed it. If you were born before the 30th
June 1940 you were in. I had to register and
go for a medical but I knew I wouldn't pass as
I have no elbow in one arm. It was later
altered to the 31st December 1939 so I
wouldn't have had to go even if I was fit.

***Did your arm handicap you later on in your
work?***
No, it never stopped me from lifting at all. I
did it at St Aidan's School. I have no elbow
underneath. They took the elbow away. It was
smashed up. I did it playing football when I
was eight or nine so I always had that bad
arm.

Did it effect your shovelling?
No, not a problem.

Tell me about policing in your community when you were a child Jim.
I spoke to a couple of policemen who were built like whippets recently. I said to them that policemen in our day were built like bloody brick shit houses.

"Well how did they run to catch criminals?" one said.

I said: "They didn't need to run because they knew everybody. The local bobby on the beat lived local too. He only had to see you from a hundred yards off. Then of a night time he'd go in the pub and tell your dad!"

It was a community then. Your local policeman doesn't even come home in his uniform now.

We're having more trouble lately than we've ever had round here. They bashed my back door in because these back doors back onto the canal towpath. I've just made a new door. They did the same to a woman's back door further down too. I don't know why they're bashing them in.

The usual line is that they are bored as there's nothing to do in the area. Well it's alright saying that. Now when we were their age we were working, don't forget, at fourteen and fifteen. It was just the same for us and we didn't have the money to spend like the kids of today but we had things to do. We had plenty to do.

Kids don't seem to play out like they did years ago why do you think that is?

From Charnley Street we had Harrison's Recreation Ground at the bottom, when you come up Hollin Bridge Street, it's on the right hand side. We used to call that the rec. That recreation ground was for girls and lads weren't allowed on there if they were over seven years old. We had to go on what we called the back field. This was strictly enforced as there was someone to keep an eye on things at the recreation ground house. At the rec we had *the red shed.* Now we could go under the shed if it was raining. You could also go on the swings at times but if any girls come you had to get off.

The ground was owned by Mrs Harrison, who built Harrison's gym, which has now been knocked down. We used to go there three nights a week from seven until nine. We would go on Monday, Wednesday and Friday. Girls used to go on Tuesdays and Thursdays because they would never let girls and boys mix.

Don't you think it was a bad thing for the sexes not to mix socially?

What the hell did they want to mingle socially for?

There was only one fellow who looked after Harrison's Gym, Mr Haddock. He lived in the end house on Herbert Street. He only had a few yards to go to his work and he looked after Harrison's and nobody else. He was the caretaker and there were two teachers who looked after the gymnasium at the bottom. You could go in if you were under a certain age from 7:00pm until 8:00pm. It was a proper big 'un. Then when you were fourteen you could use the gym from 7:00am until 9:00pm. The rest of the time you would spend playing darts and snooker upstairs. It was like a youth club with only one fellow looking after it. If you got in any sort of bother and you were told that you couldn't come the next week. That was the rule and you didn't go.

There were two places. There was Harrison's Institution. There was one for girls where they did cookery, sewing and that kind of stuff. That was in one building and the other was the gymnasium. I never went in the girls' institute. They would never let you in and you knew that you hadn't to go in.

Did you watch any television when you were younger?

The first TV that I ever saw was my Uncle Fred's. He lived in Baldwin Street. A fellow in Grimshaw Park had a wireless shop and my Uncle Fred supplied him with coal.

"I'm getting three televisions next week," he said to my Uncle Fred.

"How much are they?" said my uncle.

He wanted £90 each for them. So Uncle Fred said he'd take one. So the wireless shop owner had one, Fred got one and somebody else had the other. The sets had nine inch screens.

Laughter.

Our night was Tuesday night. This would be in 1952 or 1953. He had somebody every night bar Saturday and Sunday. Me, my mother, dad and our Fred my brother, would go every Tuesday night from 7:00pm until 10:00pm when the TV went off.

I can always remember that on a Tuesday night The War at Sea would be on for half an hour. There were also quiz shows. You had to watch in perfect darkness and every time a bus went past along Bank Top the screen went up and down as there were no suppressers on the buses.

Tell me about your work as a coalman.

Everybody I know who worked in the coal job eventually suffered from arthritis in the neck and arthritis in the bottom of the spine. That was all through getting wet. Your collar in the wet weather was always wet as the leather back only came so far and it was cut to the shape of your neck but never came up that far. The knees were always getting wet too and you would eventually suffer from arthritis in the fingers through gripping the wet bags carried on your back. In those days nobody bothered about these things because if you worked in the coal yard you were classed as the lowest of the low and it didn't matter. We got all the lads that nobody else would take on.

You had to be rough to survive in a coal yard. One man once smashed me up. He said I pinched some bloody bags and I said I hadn't. He set about me and give me a bloody good hiding. I gave out one or two good hidings myself and he gave me a good hiding, but I caught him later! If you show any sign of fear you would be picked on all the time it was a very tough game.

My dad said that there was a coal yard at Cherry Tree and at Mill Hill now I can never remember those two. I started at the coal yard at Taylor Street. Then there was Duckworth Street and King Street. There was also a coal

223

yard at Daisyfield but the Coal Board had their own place at Florence Street. There was also a coal yard at Wilpshire.

Can you remember the large cob of coal that was once on display outside a coal merchant's premises on King Street?
Yes, it was outside Crook and Thompson's. They were the biggest coal merchant in Blackburn. That piece of coal stood there for years and years. It was at Whalley Banks, facing the Pump House pub. It had curb stones round it and it was on the flags. Crook and Thompson's trademark was black diamonds. The coal was there up to the 1950s and then it was removed because people were pinching bits of it as they couldn't get coal due to rationing. They didn't take coal off ration until 1957 or '58 it was the last thing ever to be taken of ration.

Did most of your customers have a grid at the front of the house for the coal to be tipped in or did you deliver to the rear of the house?
There weren't many that had grids but there were a few on Canterbury Street - especially those that backed on to the fire station. They all had grates on Canterbury Street and I think

Freckleton Street. There weren't many with grates at the front door.

I saved a fellow's life on Canterbury Street. It was about 5:30pm or 5:45pm. I had a lad working with me and I dropped him off. I had the last five bags to deliver down this grate on Canterbury Street at a private house. It was dark, nearly pitch black. There were only little lamps to light the streets in those days, not like today. I had this grate up and it was a round one, enough for someone to have a nasty accident and fall in. I threw the first bag down and left the bag at the side of the grate. You always have to watch for anybody walking near the grate.

This young fellow was walking along and he got fairly near so I shouted: "Watch this grate pal!"

Instead of saying *alright* he never said nowt. He kept walking and went down the bloody grate! I grabbed him by the shoulders and pulled him back up He would have banged his bloody head and gone right down the hole!

Laughter.

What was his reaction when you pulled him out?

He was as white as a ghost! I thought it was a bloody ghost!

I said: "Have you got no more sense when I tells thee to watch the grate?"

Friday night and Saturday dinner time we went collecting. By the time we had finished on a Friday it was always 9:00pm to 9:30pm.

What were the occupational hazards?

It got to a stage in the winter that my hands were that bad a condition that I used to go in the pub and I wouldn't go to the bar.

I used to say to somebody: "Go and get two pints. Here, I'll pay for them."

My hands were in that bad a condition. My fingers were all cracked with the weather from the bags and the coal and I used to soak them in salt water to get some relief when I finished off. I'd fill the sink up with hot water and salt and put my hands in. My dad and our Fred never had hands like me. The rougher the weather was the harder we had to work. It was a way of life.

When it had been snowing and it was fresh on the ground, we didn't go out until other traffic had been on the road. We would hold back until perhaps dinner time. The same would be in fog. We didn't go out until it had cleared.

Some of the back yards you went in with the coal were full of bloody dog muck. You had to watch where you dropped your bag!

Laughter.

When I was a lad and I lived on Charnley Street, we had no electric upstairs. We had gas lights upstairs. We had electric in the washhouse and in the stables. They didn't bother about the house. They bothered about the animals. I have a picture of my dad and the last horse we had called Jimmy.

We were all called James in our family and my lad has broken the line really. He has a little lad who is two year old now and he's been called Benjamin James. Now everybody else was called James. My great granddad, who lived on Spring Bank Terrace, was called James and my granddad was called James. Now my dad was called James Cronshaw. His mother, my grandma Whittle, was one of the Cronshaws that built the Sessions House. They went bust building that, there were that many killed. It was built by Wilf Cronshaw.

My dad was born in 1904 so when the First World War started in 1914 he was only ten. My Uncle Fred was born in 1898 and he went to the war in 1915. Uncle Fred used to brag about what he had done, going over the top when he wasn't even eighteen and one thing and another. I don't know which regiment he was in but I still have his medals. It doesn't tell you on his medals.

Billy Shaw, my Grandma Weaver's brother, I had his medals and it said on them William Shaw and his number in The Durham Light

Infantry. Uncle Fred married but him and Aunty Annie had no children and he always wanted children. Fred took me everywhere if my dad wasn't going. He'd say *come on cock you can come with me.*

When did the family coal business start Jim?
Well my granddad was sixty when he died. He died in 1936, in Christie's Hospital, with bowel cancer. His dad started it before him so it's going back somewhere to about 1850. At the time they lived at Spring Bank Terrace. That is the first record that there is of them.
They would pick the coal up from Mill Hill Station. There's an old warehouse there. It's a stone built warehouse. The coal yard was there. There's a fencing place there now. They make fences and sheds. That's where the coal yard was. You see they couldn't travel so far due to the horses so they were always local.
When you think about it, they built the coal yard there and Waterfold Mill, which is still there and there was the other mill on the opposite side of Queen Victoria Street, where Neal's Scrap yard used to be. Now they built them factories there in the railway age so that they could move the cotton and coal and take cloth away. It could all be done on the railway and they weren't above five hundred yards away from the transport house. They did

the same in the canal age. They built the mills alongside of the canals.

This firm had a big coal yard on Audley Bridge. My dad used to say that he would have had about twelve horses out with coal but Crook and Thompson's would have about thirty. When I worked for my dad and uncles we had four motors. In those days Uncle Fred would drive a vehicle, so would Uncle Arnold and my dad. Fred my brother would look after the office.

Did you ever think that one day coal would be practically obsolete?

Well that was the trouble. We were making that much bloody money, we never even considered it would end one day. Gradually smokeless came in. Coalite had been around for a while and was made in Chesterfield. Then there was Firemax which was made by the Gas Board, I think, in Burnley, but gas and electric heating killed them all.

These smokeless fuels would be a lot lighter than coal so did it mean extra mileage for the coalman carrying the bags?

Well originally, until they stopped us, we used to put three quarters of a hundredweight in the bags. If you wanted ten hundredweight you got fourteen and ten and half hundredweight. By the early to middle seventies they came out with all these things that you couldn't have them in three quarters, they had to be in fifty kilos and twenty five kilos. You couldn't have any other weight.

When did you decide to call it a day Jim?
I finished in 1995. There was nothing left. We ended up with me and our Fred actually putting money in to pay our own wages.

Tell me about your childhood.
We had a midwife in Charnley Street called Alice Bretkle who ran a paper shop. She wasn't a real midwife but if a midwife couldn't get there she would step in. She knew everybody. She was in everybody's house. Nurse Taylor from New Wellington Street was the proper nurse but if she had someone else to look after Alice Bretkle would step in and get everything ready.
Alice used to come in our house in Charnley Street every night at 6:30pm. She'd open the front door and walk down the lobby. We'd be sat in the living room, it was a big living room, listening to the wireless. She'd greet everybody then go off into the kitchen and start washing up.
Alice would stop until about 7:45pm, have a cup of tea and a fag and then she'd be off.

Every morning at around 9:00am she would come across to our house again and two or three other women would come in and they'd sit around the fire supping tea and smoking fags, those who weren't working. Everybody knew everybody. This would be when I was a young lad in the late forties.

We used to have a little red cash book, which was for money paid to the doctor. He'd collect the money every Friday night. This was prior to the National Health Service, but he would collect money every night of the week. You paid whether you were ill or not to keep on his books.

I never remember there being a chemist until much later on. The doctor did all that. He had a dispenser working for him. The chemist shop came along later with the NHS.

Tell me about your trips to First World War battlefields.

Go to a First World War battlefield and you'll get the biggest eye opener you've ever had. You'll not know weather to be sad or mad! I've been once and I'd like to go again. We went to all the battlefields in five or six days and it's bloody good. The irony of it is all these graves are immaculate. I went in the summer so there were a lot of flowers around the graves. They were immaculate, no graffiti or anything like that.

On a grave stone it just had their name, their rank, their regiment and number. If you wanted any more words putting on the stone, the parents of the dead servicemen, or their next of kin, had to pay threepence a word. Threepence in them days was a lot of money.

It was a fantastic trip. Our guide had studied this war all his life. He was English and what he didn't know wasn't worth knowing.

My Uncle Fred went all the way through the war from 1915 and he came out without a blinking scratch on him. Little Chuck, who we all knew as Chuck, taught me to drive. He went through the war and his legs were smashed to pieces. Chuck worked in the coal yard but he was always in bloody agony. He retired when he was sixty five but he hadn't a birth certificate so his real age wasn't known. In the last year working for us all he could do was sew coal bags, as we used to sew them in those days, but he was in agony with his legs.

Chuck did all the driving when he was with me. He couldn't carry. I did all the lifting.

There were two of my dad's cousins killed in the war. I can't remember their names but my dad told me they were killed in France.

You know they still play the Last Post every night in Belgium at 8:00pm, every day of the year? The town stops and is silent while this happens - even kids playing football stop their game.

I've still got my Uncle Fred's Labour Certificate stating that he can now leave school. I had another from when he was eleven saying that he could do half a day at school and half a day at work.

Uncle Fred, my Dad and Uncle Arnold all went to Immanuel Primary School. It's not there now. It was cn Graphton Street and Wilson Street. It was knocked down about 1980. My dad never went to any other school, only Immanuel. They had a centenary or a hundred and fifty year do and my girls and my lad who also went to the school were asked for any memorabilia about the school for an exhibition that they were holding. I leant them some stuff and they never came back.

Tell me a story or two about some of the characters you have known.

I'll tell you a story about my dad who was three months short of ninety when he died. Three months before that he gave up smoking his pipe. He said that it wasn't doing his eyes any good. He was going blind and he blamed it on his pipe. He finished up not being able to walk so far. I used to take him down Pleasington, where the changing rooms are. I used to stop the car and get him out into his wheelchair and he liked to watch the football. He liked any sports.

He said to me: "See them trees?"

Now these trees were about seventy or eighty feet high and wide. You couldn't put your arms round them.

"See them trees? I remember when they were only as big as thee cock!"

I said: "Get away! Those trees will be three or four hundred years old!"

"No, they were planted in my lifetime when I were a little lad!"

I said: "This was a private estate then belonging to the Feildings. How can you say that? It wasn't a playing field then dad."

"No was it buggery a playing field. I used to sneak in here for a shortcut."

"Where were you going dad?" I said.

"Well in the summer when we didn't have any work for the horses and your granddad didn't want to pay for their food, if they weren't working, we used to take them to Pleasington at the back of Butlers Pub where there was a farm. We would put them out there all summer to graze. They lived off the grass and they stopped out all night with it being summer, so they didn't need much looking after. Your granddad would just pay the farmer a few bob for the rent.

"I used to get the job of taking them. I was only about nine. I'd be on the back of one with the reins in my hand leading another and I used to ride them from Charnley Street, down to Pleasington, along Preston Old Road, up Pleasington Lane to the farmer's up at the Butlers. Then I had to walk it home. I didn't walk all that bloody way back. I used to take a shortcut through Pleasington, along that path that were there, and I'd come back through Witton Park. I used to jump over the wall. I saw the king one day!"

I said: "We've seen the King."

He said: "Not that King that you've seen. I've seen George V! He was having a ride in his carriage around the park with Colonel Fielding. You had to be careful as the Colonel had gamekeepers. You weren't allowed in. We used to jump over that stone wall that's still there and I'd walked it back. I had to hide in the bushes so I'd not be seen, so that's how I know how long the trees have been here and all about this place."

Little Chuck, whose name was Cuthbert Cheatham, once told me that before he worked in the coal job, when he was about fourteen, he used to drive a pair of horses taking weft and cotton to and from Preston for Hawkins and Birtwistles Cotton.

To take a pair of horses to Preston and back you weren't getting home until 9:00pm. He told me that he used to get two pence bait money going and two pence bait money for coming back. The best place to stop he told me was The Royal Oak at Riley Green because she made a right good barmcake and always had a right good fire on. The horses were put in the yard with a nose bag on. Coming back one night he had to stop at The Traveller's Rest. When you were coming up Houghton Brew you couldn't ride with a pair of horses. You had to shove up at the back to tell the horses to get you up the brew. When you got to the top of the brew you'd stop and have ten minutes to give the horses a rest while you had a fag.

One night Chuck told me he was sat outside the pub when this fellow came round the corner with a knife and stuck it at his throat. He told Chuck to give him his money, so Chuck had to give him his two pence of course. When he got to The Royal Oak he had no money for a bite to eat, but he had to let the horses have a drink and nose bag.

He went in the pub for a warm and a fellow said to him: "Are you not getting a barmcake Chuck?"

He said that he had no money and told him about the man at the Traveller's Rest robbing him. This chap said I won't be a minute and went outside to his cart and came back with a knife with an eight inch blade on it.

"Here you are. That's yours. If he ever stops you again have it ready and shove it in his bloody throat!"

About three week later this fellow tried it on again but this time Chuck said he was waiting for him and held a knife at his throat. He never tried again. He still had that knife up until he retired. He used to wear it off his belt, on the inside of his pants, so it couldn't be seen.

If you would like to tell your story and
be involved in future volumes of this
work then please contact Heritage
Publications on 01254 245709 or
email Info@HeritagePublications.co.uk